Mongiwekhaya

I See You
Ngiyakubona
Ek Sien Jou
Ndiyakubona

Bloomsbury Methuen Drama
An imprint of Bloomsbury Publishing Plc

BLOOMSBURY
LONDON · OXFORD · NEW YORK · NEW DELHI · SYDNEY

Bloomsbury Methuen Drama

An imprint of Bloomsbury Publishing Plc

50 Bedford Square	1385 Broadway
London	New York
WC1B 3DP	NY 10018
UK	USA

www.bloomsbury.com

BLOOMSBURY, METHUEN DRAMA and the Diana logo
are trademarks of Bloomsbury Publishing Plc

First published 2016

British Library Cataloguing-in-Publication Data
A catalogue record for this book is available from the British Library

ISBN: PB: 978-1-4742-8811-8
ePub: 978-1-4742-8812-5
ePDF: 978-1-4742-8810-1

Library of Congress Cataloging-in-Publication Data
A catalog record for this book is available from the Library of Congress

Typeset by Country Setting, Kingsdown, Kent CT14 8ES
Printed and bound in Great Britain

THE ROYAL COURT THEATRE AND MARKET THEATRE JOHANNESBURG PRESENT

I See You

by Mongiwekhaya

I See You was first performed at the Royal Court Jerwood Theatre Upstairs, Sloane Square, on Friday 25 February 2016 and first performed at the Market Theatre Johannesburg on 13 April 2016

I See You is presented as part of International Playwrights: A Genesis Foundation Project.

Genesis
FOUNDATION

I See You

by Mongiwekhaya

CAST (in alphabetical order)

Skinn **Jordan Baker**
Buthelezi **Desmond Dube**
Ben **Bayo Gbadamosi**
James **Austin Hardiman**
Masinga **Sibusiso Mamba**
DJ Mavovo/Dr Pravesh **Amaka Okafor**
Shabangu **Lunga Radebe**

Director **Noma Dumezweni**
Designer **Soutra Gilmour**
Lighting Designer **Richard Howell**
Composer & Sound Designer **Giles Thomas**
Movement Director **Luyanda Sidiya**
Casting Director **Amy Ball**
Assistant Director **John Haidar**
International Director **Elyse Dodgson**
Associate Director (International) **Richard Twyman**
International Assistant **Sarah Murray**
Production Manager **Bernd Fauler**
Voice & Dialect Coach **Zabarjad Salam**
Fight Director **Bret Yount**
Costume Supervisor **Chris Cahill**
Stage Managers **Julia Slienger, Dan Gammon**
Stage Manager Work Placement **Elizabeth Rodipe**
Set Built by **Illusion, Design and Construct Ltd.**
Scenic Art by **James Rowse**

Mongiwekhaya wishes to thank the Cenre for Humanities Research at the University of Western Cape

I See You
by Mongiwekhaya

Mongiwekhaya (Writer)

Theatre includes: **Kagg'an Dreams (Handspring Trust); Qhawe, The Feather Collector (Grahamstown Festival).**

Mongiwekhaya is a writer and director with Handspring Trust for Puppetry Arts and presently performs in the International tour of Ubu and the Truth Commission. He is currently Artist in Residence for Center for Humanities Research (CHR) at the University of Western Cape and a member of the newly formed SA Playriot group.

Jordan Baker (Skinn)

For the Royal Court: **Brave. (Rehearsed Reading)**

Television includes: **Eastenders, Doctors.**

Desmond Dube (Buthelezi)

Theatre includes: **Julius Caesar (Nelson Mandela); You Fool How Can The Skyfall (Windybrow); Who Really Freed Nelson?, Jozi Jozi (Market/Baxter); Street Sisters (Stadsscchouwburg, Amsterdam); Scribble (Baxter); Survival (Civic); Protest (South African State Theatre); NONGOGO (Soweto/Market/Canadian Stage Theatre)**

Television includes: **Suburban Bliss, Joburg Blues, Dube on Mondays(x7), Font, No. 1 Ladies' Detective Agency, Dube Reloaded.**

Film includes: **Hotel Ruanda, Love & Broken Bones, The Long Run, Millinium Menace, Hopeville, Mandela's Gun.**

Awards include: **FNB Vita Award for Supporting Actor (Scribble); Avanti Award for Best actor in A Comedy Series (Joburg Blues); Naledi Award for Best Supporting Actor (Nongogo).**

Noma Dumezweni (Director)

This is Noma's Directorial Debut.

As Performer, for the Royal Court: **Linda, Feast (Young Vic), Belong.**

Other theatre includes: **A Human Being Died that Night (Market Theatre/Brooklyn Academy of Music/Hampstead); Carmen Disruption (Almeida); 'Tis Pity She's A Whore (Globe); A Walk on Part-The Fall of New Labour (Soho); The Winter's Tale, Julius Caesar, The Grainstore, Morte D'Arthur, Romeo & Juliet, Little Eagles, Macbeth (RSC); Six Characters in Search of an Author (Chichester Festival/West End); The Master & Margarita, Nathan the Wise, The Coffee House (Chichester Festival); The Hour We Knew Nothing of Each Other, President of an Empty Room (National); Breakfast with Mugabe (RSC/Soho/West End); A Raisin in the Sun (Lyric Hammersmith/West End/Tour); Skellig (Young Vic); Anthony & Cleopatra, Much Ado About Nothing, Henry V (West End); The Bogus Woman (Red Room/Bush).**

Television includes: **Casualty, Capital, The Marriage of Reason & Squalor, Midsomer Murders, Frankie, Doctor Who, Summerhill, The Colour of Magic, The Last Enemy, Together, Fallout, Little Miss Jocelyn, Eastenders, New Tricks, Holby City, Fallen Angel, After Thomas, Silent Witness.**

Film includes: **The Incident, Dirty Pretty Things, Macbeth.**

Awards include: **Olivier Award for Best Performance in a Supporting Role (A Raisin in the Sun); Manchester Evening News Award for Best Fringe Performer, Fringe First Award (The Bogus Woman).**

Bernd Fauler (Production Manager)

Theatre includes: **Lippy, Ah, Wilderness!, The Trial, Song From Far Away, La Musica, Bull (Young Vic); The Roundabout Auditorium (development and build management); The Angry Brigade (& tour), Jumpers For Goalposts (& tour), Good With People, Wasted, 65 Miles, Lungs, One Day When We Were Young, The Sound Of Heavy Rain (Paines Plough); Grounded (UK & European Tour), No Place To Go, Dances Of Death, Purple Heart, The Trojan Women, Sunset Baby, The Prophet (Gate); Border Force, Gateways, Gay Shame, Gross Indecency, Latitude (Duckie); Where's My Desi Soulmate, It Ain't All Bollywood, Meri Christmas, The Deranged Marriage (Rifco Arts); Glasshouse (Cardboard Citizens); Once Upon A Time In Wigan, Krapp's Last Tape, Spoonface Steinberg (Hull Truck).**

Opera includes: **Gloria- A Pigtale (The Mahogany Opera Group).**

Other events include: **SPILL Festival 2013 (Pacitti Company).**

Bernd works as a production manager on a variety of projects including theatre, contemporary performance/live art and dance as well as outdoor & site specific performances.

Bayo Gbadamosi (Ben)

Theatre includes: **Little Revolution (Almeida); Mad about the Boy (Unicorn/Bush/Young Vic/Edinburgh Fringe); Little Baby Jesus (Ovalhouse Theatre); The Gods Are Not To Blame, The Litter, Uncle Vanya (Young Vic).**

Film includes: **Swarm, Mission London.**

Soutra Gilmour (Designer)

For the Royal Court: **The Pride, Oxford Street, Country Music.**

Other theatre includes: **Hecuba (RSC); Bull (Sheffield Theatres/Young Vic/59E59, New York) Urinetown (St James/West End); Strange Interlude, Antigone, Morning to Midnight, Moon on a**

Rainbow Shaw, Double Feature in the Paint Frame, The Shadow of a Boy (National); Assassins, Merrily We Roll Along, Torch Song Trilogy (Menier Chocolate Factory); Cyrano de Bergerac (Roundabout, New York); Into the Woods (Open Air/Public, New York); The Duchess of Malfi (Old Vic); Reasons to Be Pretty (Almeida); The Night Alive, Inadmissible Evidence, Polar Bears (Donmar) Who's Afraid of Virginia Woolf? (Sheffield Crucible/Northern Stage); The Little Dog Laughed (Garrick); The Commitments, In a Forest Dark & Deep, Three Days of Rain, From Here to Eternity (West End); The Tragedy of Thomas Hobbes (RSC at Wilton's Music Hall); Plaf (West End/Teatro Liceo, Buenos Aires); The Lover & The Collection (Comedy); Our Friends in the North, Ruby Moon, Son of Man (Northern Stage); Last Easter (Birmingham Rep); Angels in America (Headlong/Lyric, Hammersmith); Bad Jazz, A Brief History of Helen of Troy (ATC); The Birthday Party, The Caretaker (Sheffield Crucible/Tricycle); Petrol Jesus Nightmare #5 (Traverse/Kosovo); Lovers & War (Strindbergs Intima Teater, Stockholm); Hair, Witness (Gate); Baby Doll, Thérèse Raquin (Citizens, Glasgow); Ghost City (59E59, New York); When the World Was Green (Young Vic); Modern Dance for Beginners (Soho); Through the Leaves (Duchess/Southwark Playhouse).

Opera includes: Opera Shots 2012 & 2013, Down by the Greenwood Side, Into the Little Hill (Royal Opera House); Carmen, Saul, Hansel & Gretel (Opera North); Anna Bolena, Don Giovanni, Mary Stuart, Cosi Fan Tutte (English Touring Opera); The Shops (Bregenz Festival); The Birds & Trouble in Tahiti (The Opera Group); El Cimarrón (Queen Elizabeth Hall); A Better Place (ENO) The Girl of Sand (Almeida Opera).

Soutra has also designed for The Jamie Lloyd Company, productions include The Homecoming, The Ruling Class, Richard III, The Pride, The Hothouse & Macbeth.

Austin Hardiman (James)

For the Royal Court: Wish.

Theatre includes: The First Man, True West, FOG (Jermyn Street); The Dead Wait (Park); A Midsummer Night's Dream (Antic Disposition); Tempest (Zip Productions/Jermyn Street); Twelfth Night (The Faction); Macbeth (Faction/Tabard American School); The Window Cleaner (Zip Productions); A Midsummer Night's Dream, Twelfth Night (Antic Disposition/Cochrane Theatre); The Dead Wait (Park/Snapdragon Productions).

Television includes: Dancing on the Edge, Somnambulant.

Film includes: Let The Die Be Cast, False Murder, The Sorrows, Phyllis, W.E, Forget Me Not, Swagger Wars, Thunder From Her Heart, Sgt Don Greenwood, Slow Down The Time, The Dark Room.

John Haidar (Assistant Director)

As Director, theatre includes: The Little Match Girl (Birmingham REP/Tour); The New Electric Ballroom (RADA); The Beauty Queen of Leenane, A Skull in Connemara, The Lonesome West (CAM FM); Macbeth (Cambridge American Stage Tour); The Hunchback of Notre Dame, The Glass Menagerie (Corpus Playroom); Romeo & Juliet, The Alchemist (ADC Theatre).

As Assistant/Associate Director, theatre includes: Photograph 51 (West End); The Changeling, 'Tis Pity She's A Whore, Antony & Cleopatra (Shakespeare's Globe); 366 Days of Kindness, Tartuffe (Birmingham REP); All's Well That Ends Well (RADA).

Richard Howell (Lighting Designer)

Theatre includes: Privacy (Donmar); The Homecoming (Trafalgar Studios); East is East (Trafalgar Studios/tour); The Crucible, The Life & Times of Fanny Hill (Bristol Old Vic); Little Shop of Horrors, A Doll's House (Royal Exchange, Manchester); Playing for Time (Sheffield Theatres); The Invisible (Bush); Jane Wenham: The Witch of Walkern (Out of Joint/Watford); Bad Jews (& West End/tour), 4000 Miles, Fifty Words, In A Garden (Theatre Royal, Bath); Les Parents Terribles, The Dance of Death (Donmar at Trafalgar Studios); Cat on A Hot Tin Roof (Northampton/UK Tour); The Recruiting Officer, Stepping Out (Salisbury); The Island (Young Vic); Jack & the Beanstalk (Lyric, Hammersmith); The Artist Man & the Mother Woman (Traverse); The Sound of Heavy Rain (Paines Plough, Roundabout); Arabian Nights (Tricycle); Uncle Vanya, Snake in the Grass (Print Room); Sherlock's Last Case, Laurel & Hardy, The Tempest, Lettice & Lovage, Great Expectations, Heroes & Single Spies (Watermill); Blue Remembered Hills, Playhouse Creatures, Fred's Diner (Chichester Festival); The Glass Menagerie (West Yorkshire Playhouse).

Opera & Dance includes: Jekyll & Hyde (Old Vic/McOnie Company); Madama Butterfly (Den Jyske Opera); Swanhunter (Opera North); Flight, Il Trittico, Madama Butterfly, La Fanciulla (Opera Holland Park); My First Cinderella, My First Coppelia (ENB); A Little Princess (London Children's Ballet); La Clemenza Di Tito (Royal Conservatoire, Glasgow); The Magic Flute (Royal College of Music).

Sibusiso Mamba (Masinga)

As Writer & Performer, theatre includes: Holiday Jubilee (Crossroads Theatre Co); Train to 2010 (University of Missouri Kansas City/Crossroads Theatre, New Jersey).

As Performer, theatre includes: The Taming of the shrew (Friargate Theatre); Sizwe Banzi is Dead (Young Vic/Eclipse); Adventures of Nhamo (Tiata Delights, Africa Centre); The Lady from Dubuque, A Taste of Honey (Lewes Little Theatre/Love&Madness); Othello, The Importance of Being Earnest (QM2) Julius Caesar (Civic Theatre, Johannesburg) Nongogo (Market Theatre, Johannesburg); Romeo & Juliet (Chichester Festival); Big Boys (Croydon Warehouse Theatre); Tartuffe, The Rocky Horror (Swaziland Theatre Club).

Television Includes: **Doctors, Society, Isidingo, Soul City.**

Film includes: **Coronation Street: Out of Africa, Crime, Wah-Wah.**

Radio includes: **When The Laughter Stops, Mandida's Shoes, 49 Donkeys Hanged, Sagila, Banana Republic, Taxi.**

Sibusiso Mamba is an actor, playwright, director, screenwriter & producer. He has co-created and written for many television series in South Africa. Sibusiso is Script Editor on the South African television show Skeem Saam and is International Associate Artist at Crossroads Theatre in New Jersey, USA.

Amaka Okafor (DJ Mavovo/Dr Pravesh)

Theatre includes: **Hamlet (Barbican/Sonia Friedman); Mermaid (Shared Experience); Bird (Root); Glasow Girls (National Theatre of Scotland/Citizens/Theatre Royal, Stratford East); The Snow Queen (& India Tour), Flathampton (Royal & Derngate, Northampton); Beauty & the Beast, The Garbage King, The Tempest, The London Eye Mystery, Cinderella (Unicorn); Dr Korczak's Example (Royal Exchange, Manchester/Arcola); Sabbat (Dukes); Branded, 24 Hour Plays, Hitting Heights (Old Vic); Robin Hood & the Babes in the Wood, Red Oleander, When Brecht Met Stanislavski (Salisbury Playhouse); Meantime (Soho); Tracy Beaker Gets Real (Nottingham Playhouse); Stamping, Shouting & Singing Home (Polka); The Alexander Projekt (Split Moon).**

Lunga Radebe (Shabangu)

As Director, theatre includes: **Heading Out (Rattlestick Playwrights Theatre, Ny); Voices – Black History Month (International House Davis Hall, Ny); Disappearing Act (Provincetown Theatre/Black Box Theatre, Ny).**

As Playwright, theatre includes: **Avalon: A New Township (Shapiro Theater, NY); Blues For Tsheleng (Genesis Festival: Crossroads Theatre, New Jersey).**

As Performer, theatre includes: **Antigone: In The World (New York/Kenya/South Africa Tour); Avalon: A New Township Play (Shapiro Theater, NY/UK Tour); Tears of Anatolia, The Seagull (Shapiro Theater, NY); The Last Pro in Yeoville (Windybrow/Grahamstown Arts Festival); Touch My Blood (Market Theatre); The Dead Politician (Macufe Festival); Much Ado About Nothing, Armed Response, Love, Crime & Johannesburg (Wits Theatre); The Blue Dress Red Roses & Scarlet Tie (Civic, South Africa); Reverse Lullabyes (Drill Hall).**

As Writer, television includes: **Rhythm City, Zone 14.**

As Performer, television includes: **Skeem Saam, Muvhango, Inzingane Zobaba, Mthunzini.com, Zero Tolerance, Backstage.**

As Performer, Film includes: **Vaya.**

Zabarjad Salam (Voice & Dialect Coach)

For the Royal Court: **Hangmen (& West End), Khandan (& Birmingham Rep), Fireworks; Liberian Girl; The Djinns of Eidgah; Death Tax (Open Court), NSFW.**

Other theatre includes: **The Commitments, Let It Be, The Mentalists, Bend It Like Beckham, Photograph 51 (West End); Dinner With Saddam (Menier Chocolate Factory); Harvey (Birmingham Rep/Theatre Royal, Haymarket); My Night With Reg (& West End), Splendour (Donmar); Speed-the-Plow, Hayfever, Saturday Night Fever, Who's Afraid of Virginia Woolf? (Theatre Royal, Bath); Future Conditional, Other Desert Cities (Old Vic); We Are Proud to Present... (Bush); McQueen, Urinetown (St James); Once a Catholic (Tricycle); The Island, Sizwe Bansi is Dead (Young Vic); Roaring Girl, The Empress, Julius Caesar, The Winter's Tale, Matilda, Much Ado About Nothing (RSC); Goodnight Mr Tom (Chichester Festival); Behind the Beautiful Forevers, The Veil, 13, The Comedy of Errors, The Animals & Children Took to the Streets, Travelling Light, Collaborators, The Last of the Hausmans, Timon of Athens, This House (National); The Emperor Self (Arcola); Zaide (Sadler's Wells/UK tour).**

Television includes: **Indian Summers, Cucumber/ Banana, Cilla, Being Eileen, Blandings.**

Film includes: **Tulip Fever, The Jungle Book, Lies We Tell.**

Luyanda Sidiya (Movement Director)

As Choreographer, Dance includes: **Pillars of Trust, Sacred Space, Kokuma, Invocation, Indlela (Dance Umbrella Festival); Ubuntu Bam (ACE Dance & Music Company); Umnikelo (Triple Dose); Dominion (Vuyani Season); Makwande (Kuopio Dance Festival, Finland); Siva (National Arts Festival).**

Awards include: **Award for Most Outstanding Dancer in Contemporary Style (FNB Dance Umbrella Festival); Decade Award for Best Contemporary Dancer (Gauteng Dance Manyano) Standard Bank Young Award for Choreography.**

Luyanda co-founded the Luthando Arts Academy for which he still works as a consultant, choreographer & teacher, & is currently the Artistic Director at Vuyani Dance Theatre. Luyanda also has danced internationally for the MIDM Company. He was dance captain for the 2010 FIFA World Cup Opening Concert.

Giles Thomas (Composer & Sound Designer)

For the Royal Court: **YEN (& Royal Exchange, Manchester), Untitled Matriarch Play (or Seven Sisters); Mint; Pigeons; Death Tax; The President Has Come To See You (Open Court), Khandan (& Birmingham Rep), Shoot/Get Treasure/Repeat (& Gate/Out of Joint/Paines Plough/National),**

The Wolf from the Door, Primetime.

As Composer & Sound Designer, theatre includes: **This Will End Badly (& Edinburgh), Little Malcolm & His Struggle Against The Eunuchs (Southwark Playhouse); Pomona (National/Royal Exchange, Manchester/Orange Tree); The Titanic Orchestra, Allie (Edinburgh Festival Fringe); Outside Mullingar (Theatre Royal, Bath); Back Down (Birmingham Rep); Lie With Me (Talawa); The Sound Of Yellow (Young Vic); Take A Deep Breath & Breathe, The Street (Ovalhouse); Stop Kiss (Leicester Square).**

As Sound Designer, theatre includes: **The Snow Queen (Southampton Nuffield/Northampton Royal & Derngate); Sparks (Old Red Lion); Orson's Shadow (Southwark Playhouse); Defect (Arts Ed); Betrayal (I Fagiolini/UK Tour); A Harlem Dream (Young Vic); Superior Donuts (Southwark Playhouse); Three Men in a Boat (Original Theatre Company, UK Tour); King John (Union); It's About Time (nabokov/Hampstead); House Of Agnes (Paines Plough).**

As Associate Sound Designer, theatre includes: **Henry IV (Donmar/tour); Henry V (Michael Grandage Company/West End); 1984 (West End/Tour).**

INTERNATIONAL PLAYWRIGHTS
AT THE ROYAL COURT THEATRE

Over the last two decades the Royal Court Theatre has led the way in the development and production of new international plays, facilitating work at grass-roots level and developing exchanges which bring young writers and directors to work with emerging artists around the world. Through a programme of long-term workshops and residencies, in London and abroad, a creative dialogue now exists with theatre practitioners from over 70 countries, working in over 40 languages, most recently Chile, Cuba, Georgia, India, Lebanon, Mexico, Palestine, Russia, South Africa, Syria, Turkey, Ukraine and Zimbabwe. All of these development projects are supported by the Genesis Foundation and the British Council.

The Royal Court Theatre has produced dozens of new international plays through this programme since 1997, most recently **Fireworks** by Dalia Taha (Palestine) in 2015, **The Djinns of Eidgah** by Abhishek Majumdar (India) and **A Time to Reap** by Anna Wakulik (Poland) in 2013, **Remembrance Day** by Aleksey Scherbak (Latvia) and **Our Private Life** by Pedro Miguel Rozo (Colombia) in 2011, **Disconnect** by Anupama Chandrasekhar (India) in 2010.

ROYAL COURT AND SOUTH AFRICA
The Royal Court Theatre has a longstanding connection to new writing in South Africa. In 1973, Sizwe Banzi is Dead by Athol Fugard, John Kani and Winston Ntshona was produced in the Jerwood Theatre Upstairs and was followed by a season of three plays in the Jerwood Theatre Downstairs. John Kani described the Court at that time as his home: "to find a theatre in the free world with the same kind of vision gave us so much hope that the world was aware of our suffering." In July 2014, exactly 40 years later, a new project was born in a new South Africa. Twelve young writers from all parts of the country were selected to take part in a two-year project, working with playwrights Leo Butler, Winsome Pinnock and International Director Elyse Dodgson supported by the British Council and Connect ZA. As a result eleven new plays for South Africa and the world were created – works that give us an insight into South African life today and the urgent concerns of a younger generation two decades after the end of Apartheid. In May 2014 six of the writers were invited to London to present their work as staged readings New Plays from South Africa: After 20 Years. In 2015 the Market Theatre in Johannesburg staged readings of all eleven plays and many of them will now have full productions in some of the country's major theatres. The writers have formed a powerful collective to support new writing in South Africa – Play Riot. I See You by Mongikewaya is celebrated as the first co-production between the Royal Court Theatre and the Market Theatre.

Established by John Studzinski 15 years ago, the Genesis Foundation works in partnership with the leaders of prestigious UK arts organisations such as the Royal Court, The Sixteen, Welsh National Opera and the Young Vic. Its largest funding commitment is to programmes that support directors, playwrights and musicians in the early stages of their professional lives.

In addition it awards scholarships to exceptional student actors at LAMDA and commissions stimulating new works, from choral compositions to light installations.

In 2015 the Genesis Foundation launched its first partnership outside the UK, funding residencies for playwrights at New York's Signature Theatre.

THE ROYAL COURT THEATRE

The Royal Court Theatre is the writers' theatre. It is the leading force in world theatre for energetically cultivating writers – undiscovered, new, and established.

Through the writers the Royal Court is at the forefront of creating restless, alert, provocative theatre about now, inspiring audiences and influencing future writers. Through the writers the Royal Court strives to constantly reinvent the theatre ecology, creating theatre for everyone.

We invite and enable conversation and debate, allowing writers and their ideas to reach and resonate beyond the stage, and the public to share in the thinking.

Over 120,000 people visit the Royal Court in Sloane Square, London, each year and many thousands more see our work elsewhere through transfers to the West End and New York, national and international tours, residencies across London and site-specific work.

The Royal Court's extensive development activity encompasses a diverse range of writers and artists and includes an ongoing programme of writers' attachments, readings, workshops and playwriting groups. Twenty years of pioneering work around the world means the Royal Court has relationships with writers on every continent.

The Royal Court opens its doors to radical thinking and provocative discussion, and to the unheard voices and free thinkers that, through their writing, change our way of seeing.

Within the past sixty years, John Osborne, Arnold Wesker and Howard Brenton have all started their careers at the Court. Many others, including Caryl Churchill, Mark Ravenhill and Sarah Kane have followed. More recently, the theatre has found and fostered new writers such as Polly Stenham, Mike Bartlett, Bola Agbaje, Nick Payne and Rachel De-lahay and produced many iconic plays from Laura Wade's **Posh** to Bruce Norris' **Clybourne Park** and Jez Butterworth's **Jerusalem**. Royal Court plays from every decade are now performed on stage and taught in classrooms across the globe.

It is because of this commitment to the writer that we believe there is no more important theatre in the world than the Royal Court.

Supported using public funding by
ARTS COUNCIL ENGLAND

ROYAL

IN 2016 THE ROYAL COURT IS 60 YEARS NEW

Until 12 Mar
Escaped Alone
By Caryl Churchill

30 Mar – 7 May
X
By Alistair McDowall

5 Apr – 7 May
Cyprus Avenue
By David Ireland
Royal Court Theatre and the Abbey Theatre
An Abbey Theatre Commission

17 May – 21 May
Ophelias Zimmer
Directed by Katie Mitchell
Designed by Chloe Lamford
Text by Alice Birch
In association with Schaubühne Berlin

18 May – 18 Jun
Human Animals
By Stef Smith

24 Jun – 9 Jul
Cuttin' It
By Charlene James
A Royal Court/Young Vic co-production
with Birmingham Repertory Theatre,
Sheffield Theatres and The Yard Theatre

1 Jul – 6 Aug
Unreachable
By Anthony Neilson

Tickets from £10. 020 7565 5000 (no booking fee)
royalcourttheatre.com

Cyprus Avenue is supported by Cockayne Grants for the
Arts, a donor advised fund of London Community Foundation

COCKAYNE **The London Community Foundation**

Innovation partner

 Coutts   ARTS COUNCIL ENGLAND **ARTS COUNCIL ENGLAND**

Sloane Square London, SW1W 8AS
🐦 royalcourt 📘 royalcourttheatre
⊖ Sloane Square ⇄ Victoria Station

COURT

ROYAL COURT SUPPORTERS

The Royal Court is a registered charity and not-for-profit company. We need to raise £1.7 million every year in addition to our core grant from the Arts Council and our ticket income to achieve what we do.

We have significant and longstanding relationships with many generous organisations and individuals who provide vital support. Royal Court supporters enable us to remain the writers' theatre, find stories from everywhere and create theatre for everyone.

We can't do it without you.

Innovation partner

Supported using public funding by
ARTS COUNCIL ENGLAND

Remember the Royal Court in your will and help to ensure that our future is as iconic as our past.

Every gift, whatever the amount, will help us maintain and care for the building, support the next generation of playwrights starting out in their career, deliver our education programme and put our plays on the stage.

To discuss leaving a legacy to the Royal Court, please contact:

Liv Nilssen, Deputy Development Director,
Royal Court Theatre, Sloane Square,
London, SW1W 8AS

Email: livnilssen@royalcourttheatre.com
Tel: 020 7565 5079

LEAVE A LEGACY

The English Stage Company at the Royal Court Theatre is a registered charity (No. 231242).

THE MARKET THEATRE

The iconic Market Theatre celebrates 40 years of story telling in 2016, founded by Mannie Manim and the late Barney Simon, and was constructed out of Johannesburg's Indian Fruit Market - built in 1913. The theatre went on to become internationally renowned as South Africa's "Theatre of the Struggle".

The Market Theatre challenged the apartheid regime, armed with little more than the conviction that culture can change society. The strength and truth of that conviction was acknowledged in 1995 when the theatre received the American Jujamcyn Award. In providing a voice to the voiceless, The Market Theatre did not forego artistic excellence, but, rather, made a point of it. Its twenty-one international and over three hundred South African theatre awards bears eloquent testimony to the courage and artistic quality of its work.

During the past four decades, The Market Theatre has evolved into a cultural complex for theatre, music, dance and the allied arts. Today, The Market Theatre remains at the forefront of South African theatre, actively encouraging new works that continue to reach international stages.

The leadership and staff remain committed to maintaining the highest possible artistic standards as it searches out exemplary new writing, and the best new, young directors, designers and lighting designers to achieve this mission.

Concerning the necessary and extraordinary act of bringing opposing forces together, these words exist because of you, my family, and you, my country. I am because we are.

I See You
Ngiyakubona
Ek Sien Jou
Ndiyakubona

FLACTAH
Flagship on Critical Thought in African Humanities

science & technology
Department
Science and Technology
REPUBLIC OF SOUTH AFRICA

NRF National Research Foundation

CENTRE FOR HUMANITIES RESEARCH
UNIVERSITY of the WESTERN CAPE

Characters

Somandla 'Ben' Mthombeni, *nineteen. Born in South Africa, raised in America, currently in second year of studies at Wits University.*

Yvette 'Skinn' Skinner, *seventeen, but tells everyone she is eighteen. A totally Zef Afrikaner girl, she recently left her boyfriend James and is in need of a place to stay.*

Melisizwe 'Shenge' Buthelezi, *fifty-five. Ex-MK soldier, currently a sergeant of the South African Police Department. Going through a messy divorce and unable to move on.*

Zulu Masinga, *thirty. Mostly interested in what he can gain financially.*

Sipho Shabangu, *fifty-seven. Ex-MK soldier turned cop who expects to move up in the police ranks and is highly aware of the media focus on cops.*

James, *twenty-seven. Has recently been dumped by Skinn, which does not sit well with him.*

DJ Mavovo, *thirty-two. Radio DJ of the Power and the Glory.*

Dr Pravesh, *works at the Chris Hani Baragwanath Hospital in Johannesburg.*

Scene One

Abandoned parking lot.

Ringtone of Johannesburg: a sonic soundscape of traditional chants and new digital TV clips and radio DJs, revving engines and the laughter of youth in freefall. This is Johannesburg on a Friday night.

'Somandla' by Mpumi.

The moon slowly rises up, cutting the darkness into the horizon of Johannesburg city in the distance. The key feature is the Nelson Mandela Bridge, lit up with all the colours of the rainbow.

In the foreground, monolithic silhouettes of buildings frame the scene and there are the markings of parking spaces on the floor of the abandoned lot.

A man, **Buthelezi***, stands centre stage, staring at the giant moon, which flickers like an old TV.*

A car's headlights light up the man, revealing he is naked except for his briefs. **Buthelezi** *turns to stare at the car, which drives off plunging him back into darkness.*

A radio booth. Inside is **DJ Mavovo***, earphones glowing, even her glasses are lit up. She is a shamanistic presence, personification of the Nelson Mandela Bridge, dancing to the music.*

DJ Mavovo   It's the weekend baby! *As'phuzeni sishaye le*[1] dance floor! This is the Power and the Glory, with your DJ Mavovo! Oh man, it is so good to finally be on air with you. 'Cause life is like . . . you know what life is like out there, anything can happen to you. But radio is therapy, and the doctor is in. Music can heal the wounds of the past and the scintillating sounds of my voice will sooth the savage beast! It's Friday night so light it up! This is your moment! Call in give us a shout out, let us know what you doing tonight.

Mavovo *dances to a fade.*

1 Let's drink and hit the . . .

The man, **Buthelezi**, *kneels in front of a bucket. He switches on the TV. He is illuminated by the screen as he washes himself, cleaning off the images as they play on his form.*

News Anchor (*on SABC 3*)   Mr Mandela's month-long hospitalisation caused a wave of anxiety across the world; but that anxiety is most palpable in South Africa, where the Nobel Peace Prize winner is seen as the father of a post-apartheid, all-inclusive –

Buthelezi *switches channels. He continues washing.*

Desmond Tutu (*on SABC 2*)[2]   Ubuntu. Ubuntu! We say this person has Ubuntu because in our culture there is no such thing as a solitary individual. We say, a person is a person through other persons.

Buthelezi *switches channels. He continues washing.*

SAP Commissioner (*on SABC 1*)[3]   . . . resist, like I said today is a day that we intend to end the violence.

Reporter   A final plea by AMCU's president Joseph Mathunjwa for workers to disperse peacefully fell on deaf ears.

Joseph Mathunjwa   We don't want any more bloodshed. We want your problems to be solved and your hopes to be realised, comrades.

Reporter   But it was not to be. Late in the afternoon, police then moved into what they called the tactical phase. It was then that the striking miners ran down the hill towards the officers.

Sounds of gunshots.

Police   Cease fire! Cease fire! Shoot you! Etc.

---

2 Desmond Tutu on Ubuntu, 'Semester at Sea', Spring 2007, <www.youtube.com/watch?v=ftjdDOfTzbk>.

3 eNCA, Marikana Massacre documentary <www.youtube.com/watch?v=sAXzs40WJ6A>.

Buthelezi *switches channels. He continues washing.*

E-TV[4]   It's Friday night! If you are looking for a fight, you've found it! Tonight on E. Skop –

Sound of a punch.

Skit –

Sound of a punch.

And donner! –

Sound of a punch.

Is action night on –

Buthelezi *switches off the TV. He starts to sing or hum.*

He towels himself off and puts on Vaseline. On his arms, on his legs. As the music begins to excite him he dances a bit, but slows down to look at his face, as he polishes it as well.

There's a furious banging at the door that stops him. He quietly gets to the bed and takes out his gun from under the pillow. Casually he walks to the door.

Buthelezi   *Ngubani loyo?*[5]

Masinga   *Wola Bhuti.*[6]

Buthelezi   *Nguban igama lakho?*[7]

Masinga   *Hhawu bhuti, uyalaz' igama lami.*[8]

Buthelezi   Do I?

Masinga   Masinga!

---

4 ETV Friday-night soundbite.

5 Who's there?

6 Hello, big brother.

7 What is your name?

8 How Buthi, you know my name.

Buthelezi   Come in.

Masinga *enters.*

Buthelezi *Sawubona Mfana.*[9]

Masinga *Nawe sawubona.*[10] Yo, it's cold out there. *Kumel' uzilungiselele.*[11]

Buthelezi *starts getting dressed.*

Buthelezi *Kunjani?*[12]

Masinga   Ah no, grand. Grand.

Buthelezi *Uhambe njani umcimbi ka Nontsikielelo?*[13]

Masinga   We went to Emmerenchia Dam, like you suggested. *Wonk'umuntu ujabulile.*[14]

Buthelezi   Good. You should save money, *that 'umdeni wakho*[15] to the countryside. *Uhambise ilizwe.*[16] See what the country really looks like without the city lights.

Masinga   Ag, when I look up I see the same stars you can see anywhere else. Soweto is enough for me.

Buthelezi   I've seen this country many times. Mostly as a soldier. But I am thinking of retiring to KZN.

Masinga   You want to leave?

Buthelezi   I am thinking about it.

9   I see you, young man.

10   I see you too.

11   You must be prepared

12   How are you?

13   And Nontsikielelo's birthday? Was it good?

14   Everyone enjoyed themselves.

15   Take your family.

16   Travel with them.

Masinga   Maybe that would be good for you.

Pause.

Buthelezi   So. Did she say anything?

Masinga   Yes.

Buthelezi   What does the woman say?

Masinga   Buthi, maybe it's time to leave this one alone –

Buthelezi   What did she say? Will she drop it?

Masinga   She's keeping the court order. If you come within a hundred metres of your house, she can have you arrested.

Buthelezi *laughs, picking up the brightly wrapped present.*

Buthelezi   Masinga. The police don't arrest the police.

Buthelezi *and* **Masinga** *exit.*

Scene Two

Skinn's *car.*

Sound of an engine starting. Lights up on an interior of a 1996 Citi Golf, and music blares from its speakers: 'Old School' by Danger Doom followed by 'Tema de amor' by Carlo Coupé. The interior of the car is a mess; torn seats with the stuffing showing, stains, packets of old McDonald's and drinks etc.

Above the car hangs the moon shifting slowly across the stage.

Ben *drives.*

Skinn *is bent over behind the chair, rummaging. She chucks up all kinds of rubbish, creating a kind of snow storm inside the car.*

Ben   Where am I going?

Skinn   Anywhere. Just drive.

Ben   We shouldn't stay out too long. I got a friend meeting me at Duke's.

Skinn *flops back on the seat, a bank bag full of weed in hand. She plops it on her lap and starts texting on her phone.*

The moon becomes **Skinn**'s *phone screen, simulating her exploration of Facebook, locating Benjamin Mthombeni and friending him.*

Skinn *types in her password.*

Skinn   You done this before?

Ben   Sure.

Skinn   Really. You have?

Ben   Ja. What do you think I am?

Skinn   Just checking.

Ben   But it's been a while.

Skinn   Oh ahh . . . now the story comes out.

Her profile page comes up with her photo, a high-angle selfie with the words SOLID GOLD *as a backdrop, written in heavy metal font. She goes to the 'search friends' engine.*

Ben   The last time was last year. My friends Kegs and Arthur came over. We hit a six-foot bong for twenty minutes, my mind was blasted.

Skinn *finds* **Ben**'s *page. His picture has him with friends, all pulling zap signs. His latest status update says: 'Oh Sh!t, Was That Today? – my autobiography.'*

Skinn *laughs at the status.*

Ben   What? What you looking at?

Skinn   Hey stop backseat browsing. What were you saying?

Ben   Okay. Um so after we cleaned out the fridge, my mom called. I said hey mother dearest. What's up? / She said I'm just checking in, everything alright? / Delightfully exquisite, I say what's up? / Everything okay she asks. / I say I'm sitting under the shimmering ocean of life just riding the currents how are you? / What did you say Benjamin? / Mom I'm walking the cat, I just told you, I'm walking a pig, oh look a beautiful flower!

Skinn   You're kidding, right?

Ben   Then she asks me, are you sober? / I say no, are you? / Benjamin Mthombeni, what are you doing?! / Mom, I'm sitting in the bathtub. Sober up and come home. I miss you. / Benjamin, you are grounded young man! / I say I know, I know. But once you sober up and live above the influence, you will see that crack is wack and Mary Jane is beautiful. Please love me.

Skinn *giggles. Above, on the screen, she clicks on 'Send Friendship Request' to* **Ben**'s *profile picture.*

Then she starts rolling a joint with the weed in the bankie.

Skinn   My first time, like proper proper? It was a Sunday and I had this roommate who gives me chronic. All I did was watch E-TV with this programme called *How They Do That with Rubber*. The one clip was this huge factory of wooden hands, and they sprayed rubber on them to make rubber gloves.

Ben   Okay.

Skinn   And they end it off with a question: How do you think they make condoms?

Ben (*laughing*)   That's crazy.

Skinn   Sent you a Facebook request.

Ben   Ja?

Skinn   Ja, so don't be a douchebag and not friend me.

Ben   How many friends you have?

Skinn   How many do you have?

Ben   Mmm about 450 or so.

Skinn   3,785.

Ben   You do not have 3,000 friends. You have a bad case of FOMO.

Skinn   Hashtag popular, babe.

Ben   Are you one of them antisocial networkers, Skinny?

Skinn   I speak to most of them. And people call me Skinn. Not Skinny, or Skank –

Ben   Skank.

Skinn *punches him in the arm.*

Skinn   Skinn!

Ben   Skinn. Got it. Is that the name your father gave you?

Skinn   *Ek het nie 'n Pa nie.*[17]

Ben   What?

Skinn   Your folks really call you Ben?

Ben   My mom called me Benjamin, yes.

Skinn   Isn't that like, an English name? A white man's name?

Ben   It's just a name.

Skinn   I know. It's interesting how people get their names, though. Like a psychic tattoo.

Ben   Well, she could have called me Benyamin which means 'Son of my Sorrow' so . . .

Skinn   I don't get it.

Ben   It's a Bible reference. Rachel named her twelfth son Benyamin and then she died. Her husband changed it to

17 Don't have a father.

Benjamin. Probably because it would be too depressing to keep saying 'Hey, Son of my Sorrow, fetch me a beer.'

Skinn   You're one of them book-smart guys, hey.

Ben   Suppose you're gonna tell me you're street smart, hey.

Skinn   What if I am?

Ben   Whenever I hear 'street smart', all I hear is someone who knows where the best drug dealers are.

Skinn *punches* **Ben** *in the arm, which causes him to swerve on the road.*

Ben   Flip, what you doing?!

Skinn   Asshole.

Ben   What's your real name? I'll find out on Facebook.

Skinn   No you won't. *Ek Skryf nooit die waarheid van myself daar nie.*[18]

Ben   I don't understand what you're saying.

Skinn   You don't speak Afrikaans?

Ben   Never learned. What did you say?

Skinn   Ach, nothing important. So . . . where do you stay?

Ben   On campus. In the res.

Skinn   Ja? They let you have sleepovers?

Ben   No, they don't. But people do anyways.

Skinn   And this friend. What's her name?

Ben   Ahhh . . . Dineo. She's a friend.

Skinn   Friend, ja. You said that. You two fuckin'?

Ben   Uh, no.

---

18 I never put anything real about me on there.

Skinn   You gay?

Ben   That's, that's just, I don't even want to qualify that with an answer.

Skinn   Qualify with an answer . . . ? What fuckin' language is that?

Ben   Look fine. Cards on the table. We doing that?

Skinn   Ja. Let's.

Ben   I'm looking to get laid.

Skinn *laughs at him.*

Ben   What's so funny?

Skinn   *Ek dink ek het jou vasgepen.*[19] This 'friend' Dineo is at Wits like you, and you quasi-asked her out to go to Duke's.

Ben   I didn't quasi-ask her out –

Skinn   So you arrive and she's not there. Probably stood you up. Am I right? I am! Ha! You bought a beer so you wouldn't look awkward. What to do? All alone. The music pumping. The crowd jumpin'. You're alone. For an hour. Twerking.

Ben   I was not twerking!

Skinn   It's hard to tell with your African ass. It shakes like jello when you sneeze.

Ben *stops the car and turns to* **Skinn**.

Ben   Jeezus, you're a son of a female dog.

Skinn   You mean bitch? You want to go back? Drop me off at a street corner and speed off?

Ben   You know what? No. Definitely not.

Skinn   You fuckin' weird, man.

19 I think I got you pinned.

Ben   Is that a good or a bad thing?

Skinn   *Jy kan regtig nie afrikaans verstaan nie,*[20] hey?

Ben   Uh –

Skinn   *Moenie strees nie. Dis beter so. Jy is so 'n opregte oukie neh?*[21]

Ben *can hear it's a question, but he doesn't know what the question is. He takes a chance and nods slowly.* **Skinn** *nods with him.*

Skinn   *Ja. Jy is. Ek het nie plek om te bly vanaand nie. Kan ek by jon bly?*[22]

Ben   Stop messing with me.

Skinn   *Jy kan my maar nou soen. Or is jy 'n virgin?*[23]

Ben *understands virgin. He kisses her.*

Skinn   Hey asshole, who said you could kiss me?

Ben   I uh . . . I thought –

Skinn *laughs.*

Skinn   You are way too easy. And yes, I expect lobolla.

She pulls **Ben** *to her and kisses him.*

Ben   Lobolla?

Skinn   Oh ja. You think a hard body like this comes cheap? Twenty cows and not a hoof less.

Ben *kisses* **Skinn**.

Ben   I'll pay for damages.

20 You really can't understand Afrikaans?

21 Don't worry about it. Its better this way. You're such a nice boy, aren't you?

22 Yes. You are. I need a place to stay tonight. Can I stay with you?

23 You should kiss me now. Or are you a virgin as well?

Skinn   Why damages?

Ben   'Cause after being with me, you'll be damaged goods.

He goes to kiss her again but **Skinn** *pushes him off.*

Ben   What?

Skinn   That's not funny.

Ben   It was a joke.

Skinn   A joke's funny. That was not funny.

Ben   Virgin isn't funny either.

Skinn   Ja. I know. That's a serious problem for a nineteen-year-old.

Ben   You gonna cure me?

Skinn*'s phone starts ringing. Her ringtone: 'Heart of Glass' by Blondie.*

Skinn   The timing couldn't be better.

Skinn *digs around her bag.*

Ben   What is that?

Skinn   My phone. Which raises a question of etiquette. Should I answer it? Or shouldn't I?

She brings out the phone.

Ben   Well?

Skinn *cancels the call.*

Skinn   *Niemand spesiaal nie.*[24] Where were we?

They kiss. **Skinn***'s phone rings again. They don't stop kissing. She switches it off, drops the phone in her bag.*

She pushes **Ben** *back, holds up the rolled joint.*

24 No one special.

Skinn   Shall we smoke? It's Swazi gold.

Ben   Colour me in.

Skinn (*laughs*)   Colour you in? You make that *kak*[25] up yourself?

Blue police car lights flash at them and the sound of the sirens. **Ben** *nervously starts driving again.*

Skinn   Oh kak, man. Shit.

Ben   Shouldn't have stopped in the middle of the road.

He reaches over, takes the joint from **Skinn**'s *mouth and chucks it out the window.*

Skinn   *Wat Doen Jy?*[26]

Ben   Chuck the bag out the window.

Skinn   What?

Ben   Chuck it. We'll come back for it.

Skinn   *Weetjy hoeveel kos hierdie zol?*[27]

Skinn *shoves the weed into her underwear.*

Ben   Speak English. This isn't a time to mess with me.

Skinn   You haven't been drinking too much, ja?

Ben   Had, uh . . . had a beer but I should be fine.

Skinn   Then we're fine.

Ben   There's nothing else lying around right?

Skinn   Yes. No. Shouldn't fuckin' be.

Ben   Shouldn't be? You're not sure?

25 Shit.

26 What are you doing?

27 You know how much this skunk costs?

Skinn   Pull over, Ben, it'll be fine.

Ben   Turn on the light and just double check.

Skinn   It's fine, pull over.

Ben   You need to be sure.

Skinn   Come on, Ben, we won't go to jail for a couple heads of weed on the floor.

Ben   I'm a law student. You know what happens if I get a record?!

Skinn   Pull over, you're making them nervous!

Ben *pulls over.*

Skinn   Relax. I've been in this kind of situation before. Don't say anything. I'll do the talking.

From the bright lights a figure approaches, dressed in a uniform of the South African Police Department. It is **Masinga**.

Masinga   Good evening, ladies and gentlemen.

Ben/Skinn   Evening, officer.

Masinga   May I enquire as to why you didn't stop driving when you saw me flashing the lights?

Skinn   We were on our way to a garage –

Masinga   Excuse me, madam, but I am speaking to the gentleman.

Ben   Um . . . like she says. We were heading to the garage to buy some Red Bull.

Masinga   Red Bull?!

Ben *nods.*

Masinga   *i-Redbull nama condom! Uplen'ukumshaya ne? 15 love engathi udlali tennis?* [28] Game?

---

28 Red Bull and condoms! You planning to hit this girl 15–love?

Ben   Sorry, officer, I speak English.

Masinga   You speak English. What is your name?

Ben   Benjamin.

Masinga   Just Benjamin?

Ben   Benjamin Mthombeni.

Masinga   Mthombeni! So you are South African? *Yini awukhulumi? Oa bua? Uyathetha?*[29]

Skinn   Officer, is there something you are looking for specifically? We'd like to be on our way.

Masinga   Madam, I am talking to the gentleman here. Please.

He puts a finger to his lips.

Mthombeni. Why don't you speak Zulu? *Ukhuluma lwimi lini?*[30]

Ben *stares at him and then shrugs dramatically.* **Masinga** *shrugs with him.*

Masinga *starts laughing and* **Ben** *joins him.*

Masinga (*shouts to the police van*)   Ye Bhuti! *Kuno Cheeseboy lapha!* [31]

Uthi uwu Mthombeni, kodwa akakwazi ukukhuluma![32]

Buthelezi   *Udakiwe?*[33]

Ben   Officer, here's my licence.

29   What mother tongue do you speak?

30   What language do you speak?

31   We have a cheeseboy here!

32   He's Mthombeni but says he doesn't speak any African language!

33   Is he drunk?

Masinga *holds his hand up.*

Masinga   Please. We'll get to that.

Skinn   Ben, just shut up.

Buthelezi *arrives.*

Buthelezi (*to* **Masinga**)   *Vula iscapha.*[34]

Masinga *walks away.*

Buthelezi   Please step out of the car, Mr Mthombeni.

Ben *gets out.*

Buthelezi   If you follow that gentleman there we will go to the station and check you quickly.

Skinn   Is that really necessary, officer?

Buthelezi   Madam, yes, it is necessary. We have no breathalyser kits here. Mr Mthombeni? Please.

Ben *walks towards the flashing police lights.*

Buthelezi   Madam, do you have a licence?

Skinn   Yes.

Buthelezi   You may follow us with your car.

Skinn   Alright. Hey, can we chat? Come over here.

She points to her window. **Buthelezi** *walks around the car to her side.*

Skinn   *Praat jy afrikaans?*[35]

Buthelezi   *Ek praat Afrikaans.*[36]

Skinn   *So, daar is 'n mis verstand hier –* [37]

34 Open the back.

35 You speak Afrikaans?

36 I speak Afrikaans.

37 So, there's been some misunderstanding here.

Buthelezi   I understand everything.

Skinn   Of course you do. *Maar, hierde situasie het hand uitgeruk uit.*[38] I mean, shit, ja we made a mistake *maar daar is geen rede om dit so ver te laat gaan nie.*[39] You get me?

Buthelezi   What mistake have you made?

Skinn   I think we should solve this here and now: What's it gonna take to make this go away?

Buthelezi   Go away?

Skinn   Ja. You know, how much for us to get in our car, you in yours, you drive south, we drive north?

Buthelezi   Is this a bribe?

Skinn   A bribe, no, I'm just, you know, I'm offering to buy a cool drink.

Buthelezi   Oh! You mean cool drink. A little something I can take to my kids.

Skinn   Ja. Look we both know how this works. Lots of paperwork for such small inyana problems. We're just some kids. Nobody's around to see anything. So why not just solve this now, make a bit of cash and we can all get on with our lives.

Buthelezi   A cool drink.

Skinn   Exactly. Everybody wins.

Buthelezi   Everybody wins.

Pause.

You have it on you now?

Skinn   Ja no. But I can get it.

---

38 But this situation has gotten out of hand.

39 But there's no need to let it go this far.

Buthelezi   Then go get it.

Skinn   Great. What police station are you from?

Buthelezi   Parkview.

Skinn   I'll see you at the station, officer.

She exits.

Buthelezi *goes to* **Ben** *and* **Masinga**.

Buthelezi   Did you hear that?

Masinga   Ja. Nothing wrong with a bit of cool drink right?

Buthelezi   You are never satisfied. (*To Ben.*) That your girlfriend?

Ben   We're friends.

Masinga   Men and women are never just friends. There's always something else going on.

Ben   We're just friends.

Buthelezi   Into the back.

Ben *hops into the back of the police van.*

Buthelezi   Mr. Mthombeni. I just want you to know that everything that happens to you tonight is to teach your 'friend' a lesson.

He slams the door on him.

Scene Three

Lollipop Lounge.

Thumping sounds of a strip club. **James** *comes out. Calls* **Skinn**.

Skinn (*voicemail*)   I might . . . Call you back.

James   Aweh, Skinn. I'm not angry any more, so why don't you calm down and answer the fuckin' phone.

Pause.

Ach man. Sorry. Everything's messed up over here. Trisha called Lolly. He's coming over. I'll talk to him about you getting off the pole and behind the bar. But what's between you and me, is between you and me. You're supposed to be at work!

Pause.

And really I'm sorry. You know what? Take the night off. Cool your head. I'll see you at sunrise.

Scene Four

Police office.

Buthelezi *enters and throws the red present on to a cramped desk.* **Masinga** *follows.*

Buthelezi (*to* **Ben**)   Sit there.

Ben *sits down.* **Shabangu** *enters and stops in front of* **Buthelezi**.

Masinga (*to* **Shabangu**)   Hey Major! I heard the news! Congratulations!

Masinga *shakes* **Shabangu***'s hand.*

Shabangu   Thank you, Masinga.

Buthelezi *stares at* **Shabangu**.

Masinga   Coffee?

Shabangu   No thank you.

Buthelezi   Yes.

Masinga *exits.*

Masinga (*off*)   Hola gents. *Uma i-coffee liphelile ukhon' ozoboshwa!*[40]

---

40 The coffee pot better be filled or I'm going to arrest someone.

Buthelezi   Major Shabangu. *Kuhamba kanjani?*[41]

Shabangu   Lieutenant, I am earning my bread. Signing forms and looking pretty for the cameras.

Buthelezi   Cameras?

Shabangu   Ja. These days everyone is always watching. *Sihlala sibhekiwe.*[42]

Buthelezi   Speaking of private –

Shabangu *holds out a letter.*

Shabangu   Here.

Buthelezi   What's this?

Shabangu   It's a letter, explaining why I can no longer help you. I've done my best for you Melisizwe. I'm sorry but there is nothing more I can do.

Buthelezi   You promised me.

Shabangu   Meli, just –

Buthelezi   You said you would speak to her, Sipho.

Shabangu   It's Major Shabangu, Sergeant. Your superior officer. Soon to be promoted to Sector Commander. Everyone is on the scanners talking about it. Local media is calling, Whatsapps from friends, Twitter's gone crazy. Ngapha ama-Facebook! Strangers want to be my friend. I have family SMSing from the *kwazula Natal.*[43] Some of them have to climb a mountain to get a signal. All saying: congratulations. Except you. My oldest friend.

He points to the present.

Is that for me?

41 How goes with you?

42 We are always being watched.

43 Eastern Cape

Buthelezi   No.

Shabangu   No. I didn't think so. Did you buy me a cake? Anything? No. I don't know why I put up with this.

Buthelezi   Congratulations, Major. Well deserved.

Shabangu   Thank you.

Buthelezi   Better pay, better hours, better life.

Shabangu   I worked hard for it.

Buthelezi   I'm happy for you.

Shabangu   Was that so hard?

Silence.

There will be no peace in this station until you have said what you need to say. So. Go ahead.

Buthelezi   Let me be clear. I need to see Tina. But you are making it very difficult for me to do that.

Shabangu *holds a hand to stop* **Buthelezi**.

Shabangu (*indicating* **Ben**)   Who is this?

Buthelezi   Don't worry about him. He's a coconut that one.

Shabangu   *Yini, akakhulumi isintu?*[44]

Buthelezi *shakes his head.*

Shabangu   *Manje khulum' isiZulu ke!*[45]

Buthelezi   Yes of course.

Shabangu   *Mfowethu, ayisekho into engayiyenza.*[46]

44 He doesn't speak.

45 Then speak Zulu.

46 Brother, there's nothing more I can do.

Buthelezi   *Ngumfazi wami.*[47]

Shabangu   She is a citizen of South Africa first.

Buthelezi   *Ukabanga ukuthi ungubani yena?*[48]

Shabangu   *Pasop (Qaphela), Buthelezi.*[49]

Buthelezi   Can you give me a run-down feedback as to what –

Shabangu   IsiZulu.

Buthelezi   *Utheni ke?*[50]

Shabangu   *Yazi Shenge, mina angisazi miselanga ukukhuluma ngalendaba.*[51] I tried to convince her otherwise, I've done my best for you. But she went ahead, the court approved it and I must enact the law to the letter.

Buthelezi   *Ungumkami Shabangu!*[52]

Shabangu (*indifferent*)   *Uthi bowumhlukumeza lomuntu!*[53]

Buthelezi   It's just marital problems –

Shabangu *holds a finger to his lips.*

Shabangu   *Awuyehlis' izwi lakho.*[54]

Buthelezi   *Ngumkami –*[55]

Shabangu   Not for much longer –

47 She is my wife.

48 Who does she think she is, treating me like this?

49 Careful, Buthelezi.

50 What has she said?

51 Listen Shenge, I'm not interested in having this discussion.

52 She is my wife, Shabangu.

53 She is claiming you abused her. That you hit her.

54 Lower your voice.

55 She is my woman –

Buthelezi   This is uncalled for! It's a private affair –

Shabangu   Lieutenant! Calm down! I understand where it is you are coming from. But this temper of yours – these days, there is no such thing as a private affair.

Buthelezi   Come now. This is not the first time we've had to be creative with the rules. Correct me if I'm wrong, but you had a minor indiscretion with those RDP houses that I helped you deal with.

Shabangu   Are you threatening me, Melisizwe?

Buthelezi   I am just saying we have solved similar problems in the past.

Pause.

Shabangu   Bhuti, the police must appear to be on her side.

Buthelezi   You owe me.

Shabangu   I think you will remain a lieutenant for ever. You have no taste for politics. Did you watch the news? That mess in Marikana? Thirty-four people gunned down. I don't know if we can recover from that. Our hand is in the fire. We must not draw attention to ourselves.

Buthelezi   I can't lose her.

Shabangu   Have you gone for the trauma counselling? Have you?

Buthelezi   Trauma counselling is for white people.

Masinga *opens the door in the hallway. He's laughing with the shadows. He has two cups of steaming coffee. He closes the door in the hall and enters the office.*

Shabangu   I wash my hands of all of this. If she does not surrender to you, then it is blood. Your blood.

Buthelezi   She will surrender.

Masinga *hands* **Buthelezi** *a cup of coffee.*

Shabangu   You better see her tonight. I can delay the restriction order till the morning. You have until then to convince her that your marital problems are a private affair and have nothing to do with the police.

Buthelezi   That's all I need. A chance to speak my mind.

Shabangu *stands up to go. He indicates to* **Ben**.

Shabangu   *Manje lona?*[56]

Masinga   Drunk driver.

Ben   I'm not drunk sir –

Buthelezi *and* **Masinga** *(to* **Ben**)   Quiet man! Shut up! *Thula! voetsek wena maan!*

Shabangu   Good. Good. I'll leave you to it.

Buthelezi   Sector Commander? *Siyabonga.*[57]

Shabangu   I am not Sector Commander just yet. Tomorrow afternoon I will be having lunch with senior Gauteng management.

Masinga   Don't forget those of us who knew you before.

Shabangu   I will be in my office if you need me. (*To* **Buthelezi**.) Good luck. Make sure tonight is the end of it.

Shabangu *exits.*

Masinga *smiles at* **Ben**.

Masinga   Hey, cheeseboy? Howzit goin', man? You cool, cheeseboy? Real cool, neh?

Ben   I'm not a cheeseboy.

Masinga   He's not a cheeseboy. (*Sniffs* **Ben**.) But he smells like Gouda.

56 And this one?

57 Thank you.

He laughs.

Ben   What's a cheeseboy?

Masinga   It's a boy who grows up with cheese in the house. You see some people have bread with butter and maybe some jam for lunch. But then a cheeseboy comes from a house with money, so he has cheese on his bread. Do you have cheese on your bread?

Ben   Yeah. And sometimes I have bread with cold meat.

Masinga *laughs and claps.* **Buthelezi** *chuckles into his coffee.*

Buthelezi   Where do you stay, cheeseboy?

Ben   At Wits University.

Buthelezi   At the University. I don't even know someone from there. You know where I stay?

Ben   No.

Buthelezi   Alexandra township. Gomorrah. *Lapho Kukhona amagundene.* Where there's all kinds of rodents. Do you know anyone from there?

Ben   No.

Masinga   *Hhawu, uyambona nje ukuthi ungu-cheeseboy lo. Akaz' aye elokshini.*[58]

Buthelezi   What are you doing with that white girl?

Ben   She's . . . she's a friend.

Masinga   A friend? (*Laughs.*) Come on, cheeseboy, you are playing. I don't know any black man who is just friends with a girl. Maybe with a sister or your mother – is she your mother?

Ben   Listen, are you going to charge me with something?

58 It's obvious he's a cheeseboy this one. Probably never gone to e'loc'tion.

Buthelezi   Oh yes.

Masinga   Yes, but don't rush it.

Buthelezi   We are definitely going to charge you.

Masinga   Definitely.

Ben   Okay, because legally I have a right to know what I'm being charged for.

Buthelezi   Oh? So you are a lawyer too?

Ben   I'm in my first year of studies.

Buthelezi   Okay. So you understand that as of right now, whilst you are studying, I am in fact a practitioner of the law.

Ben   I understand –

Buthelezi   And you? You don't know anything. When you are in school, you don't have any experience of life. Someone must put things in your head to help you. You understand me? You know nothing.

Ben   I know nothing.

Buthelezi   Yes. You know nothing.

Ben   Okay.

Buthelezi   You agree?

Ben   I understand –

Buthelezi   Good. Good. There's nothing more to say.

He opens the file on his desk and draws out a form.

Ben   What is that?

Buthelezi   Sign here.

He holds out a pen and points to a spot on the form.

Ben   Can I read the form?

Buthelezi   Sign here.

Ben   I can't sign my name to something I haven't read.

The pen is still held out.

If I could read –

Buthelezi   Okay.

He signs the form himself.

Masinga, you are my witness that he refused to sign –

Ben   I haven't refused –

Masinga   *Hhawu bhuti sizo hlal'ubusuku bonke nale s'phukuphuku?*[59]

Buthelezi *stares at* **Masinga**.

Masinga   I have witnessed that.

Ben   Just let me read –

Buthelezi   Because you have failed to understand what is expected of you in these circumstances, it is our duty to escort you to the nearest hospital and have your blood examined –

Ben   Not without my consent.

Masinga*'s phone rings.*

Masinga *ringtone: 'Dlala Mapantsula' by Tkzee.*

Buthelezi   You think you know better than me about how the law works?

Masinga *answers his phone.*

Masinga   Ola Orion! Mr Business.

Ben   Look. I think we've gotten off on the wrong foot.

Masinga   Yes, we are out tonight.

Buthelezi   Masinga.

59 How Bhuti. Are we going to spend the night with this one?

He waves **Masinga** *away.*

Masinga   You need a pick-up?

He exits.

Buthelezi   You were saying something about our feet being wrong?

Ben   Yes. I don't know what my friend Skin said to you –

Buthelezi   Skin? Skin is her name?

Ben   Yes.

Buthelezi   Is that a first or surname?

Ben   I don't know.

Buthelezi   You don't know?

Ben   That's what she calls herself. Look, officer. The point is, I'm not drunk, I'm not high or anything. I'm perfectly sober. Can't we conclude this quickly? Breathaliser check and I go home?

Buthelezi   I'd like to do that. It would have been my pleasure. But these procedures are such that you don't understand. Now these actions must come forward to their own conclusions.

Pause.

Ben   What does that form say?

Masinga *enters.*

Masinga   Hey Bhuti. *U-Orion ushoda nge-stuff e-sunrise bar.*[60] He has a package for us to pick up at Cresta, from the usual house.

Buthelezi   Ja, fine. After the blood test.

Masinga *(into phone)*   We can get it to you by midnight.

60 Orion's short at the Sunrise Bar.

He hangs up.

Ben What does the form say?

Buthelezi *gets up.* **Masinga** *and* **Buthelezi** *walk out of the room.*

Scene Five

Dr Pravesh's *office.*

Buthelezi *and* **Masinga** *stand.* **Ben** *is seated in the lights of a doctor's office.*

Dr Pravesh, *a woman in her thirties, dressed in the standard green uniform with a white coat, comes in. She turns away to shout down the hall.*

Pravesh Can we please get a cleaning lady down here! This is the second time I've nearly seen my ass slipping on this vomit!

She sees **Buthelezi**.

Pravesh Oh God. I mean, evening, officer. Sorry. Friday-night emergency room. Always starts early and ends late. No offence but you ever consider taking these cases to the private hospitals, they got the time.

Buthelezi Doctor, I'm sorry to bother you –

Pravesh *checks in a file for the correct paperwork.*

Pravesh Skip all that. Paramedics coming in with a head-on collision, three of the passengers in critical, I don't have much time. Jeezus I gotta go private.

She looks at **Ben**, *not as a person but another problem to solve.*

Pravesh Drugs or drink?

Buthelezi Drink.

Pravesh *puts on latex gloves.*

Pravesh   Simple enough. (*To* **Ben**.) You sir, Mr . . .

Buthelezi   Mthombeni.

Pravesh   Mr Mthombeni, do you consent to having your blood taken and tested for use of alcohol?

Ben   Doctor, I'd like to consent but my rights have been abused. I've been mistreated by the uniformed officer. A form was signed without my knowledge of what was on it, I was subjected to reckless driving during the ride from Linden to – where are we?

Pravesh   Officer, is this a joke?

Buthelezi   Doctor –

Ben   My rights have been abused, Doctor.

Pravesh (*to* **Buthelezi**)   Officer, I can't touch his blood without his consent.

Pause.

Intercom   Dr Pravesh to the E.R. Dr Pravesh to the E.R.

Pravesh   They're singing my song. 'Scuse me.

Pravesh *leaves.*

Buthelezi *grabs* **Ben**.

Buthelezi   I think you have a hard time listening. Didn't we agree that you know nothing?

Ben   I know I've been mistreated.

Buthelezi   You haven't been mistreated.

He slugs him through the face. **Ben** *falls to the floor.*

Buthelezi   Now you've been mistreated.

He lifts **Ben** *up.*

Masinga *comes over.*

Masinga   Easy, Bhuti, not through the face.

Buthelezi   Mr Mthombeni has not consented to a blood test.

Masinga   Why not?

Buthelezi   I blame myself. These educated ones are often the most stupid. (*To* **Ben**.) Dr Pravesh is a very nice doctor. One of the better ones. So when you embarrass me like that I get angry.

Masinga   We're supposed to pick up the package in forty-five minutes.

Buthelezi   That will have to wait.

He opens the back of the van.

Mr Mthombeni seems to think he is in charge.

Ben   I know my rights, you can't –

Buthelezi *slams his fist into* **Ben***'s belly.* **Ben***'s legs give out and he sinks against* **Buthelezi***.*

Buthelezi   Alright. It's alright, I got you. Up you go.

He and **Masinga** *help* **Ben** *into the back of the van.*

Ben *is lying horizontal, wedged under what looks like a bench, swaying and squeaking. Behind him we can see the shadows of* **Buthelezi** *and* **Masinga***, driving.*

Skinn *calls* **Ben***.*

Ben*'s ringtone: 'A Fistful of Dollars' by Ennio Morricone.*

Ben   Skinn.

Skinn   Ben. Where the hell are you? What's happening?

Ben   I think I'm in trouble.

Skinn   Ja. You just figured that? I'm at Parkview police station.

Ben   I was never at the Parkview. We were at Linden police station.

Skinn   Linden. Asshole lied to me. I'm on my way.

Ben   I'm not there any more. He took me to a hospital, he assaulted me, Skinn.

Skinn   Okay, which hospital?

Ben   He hit me! I mean, what? And the doctor –

Skinn   Ben –

Ben   The doctor didn't care!

Skinn   Are you on the way back?

Ben   Yes, I think.

Skinn   Hold on, hold on.

Ben   Do you know how fast he's driving?

Skinn   Ben –

Ben   He must be doing 120! There's no seat in the back of the van!

Skinn   They do that to soften you up. Ben, focus for me.

Ben   What?

Skinn   Why do you have your phone?

Ben   How should I know? Why would they take it away?

Skinn   They would take it and everything you have on you, if they had officially arrested you.

Ben   Does that matter?

Skinn   Yes, it matters.

Ben   We're stopping.

Skinn   You back at the police station?

Ben   No. I don't know where we are.

Skinn   Can you see a street address? What do the buildings look like –

Ben There's just trees. Skinn, they're getting out of the car.

Skinn Put the phone in your pocket, keep me with you.

Scene Six

Abandoned parking lot.

Lights rise on the police van parked near a street lamp. There are looming shadows of empty buildings. Above the Moon continues its journey. Far in the distance, the Nelson Mandela Bridge burns with all the colours of the rainbow in the midst of the fallen stars that is the city of Johannesburg. This is the middle of nowhere. We have returned to the abandoned parking lot.

Buthelezi *and* **Masinga** *step out,* **Ben** *steps out of the van. From the police car radio: DJ Cleo-Tira-Mzi, 'Kwaito House'.*

Ben Where are we?

Buthelezi My mother's house.

Ben *looks around confused.*

Ben It's a parking lot.

Buthelezi When I was a child, this was my mother's living room. Over here, we had one couch facing the radio. We were the only family in our area with this thing so neighbours used to come around, sit on the floor to listen what is happening in the world. What do you think of the place?

Ben I'd fire your architect.

Buthelezi *(chuckling)* I did. With some help. Vervoerd is dead. He took my mother's house but we won the parking lot.

Ben Are you . . . are you going to shoot me?

Buthelezi For not consenting for a blood test? Come on. Do I even have a gun on me? Look at me. Masinga is armed, though. Show him Masinga.

Masinga *pats the gun at his side.*

Buthelezi   I keep mine in the bakkie. I'm very good at it but the wife doesn't like me armed with a gun.

Ben   Why are we here?

Buthelezi   We are here because I assumed you knew how to follow simple instructions. I was wrong.

Ben   I'm just trying to exercise my rights.

Buthelezi   Shush, shut up now. The rights you have are the ones I give you. That should be clear to you, given your current circumstances. Don't fool yourself with me. See me as I am. There's no bureaucrat here. Paperwork and red tape mean nothing. There's only you and me.

Ben   I'm sorry you had such a tough life. That doesn't give you the right –

Buthelezi *punches* **Ben** *in the belly.*

Ben, *still struggling for breath, tries to crawl away from* **Buthelezi**, *who follows.*

.**Buthelezi**   I don't need your sorries, white boy. Yes. You heard right. You know white people think we are the same? We both look black. But only one of us is black.

Ben   Why you doing this?

Buthelezi *places the handcuffs in front of* **Ben**.

Buthelezi   The fact that you don't know why? That's all the reasons you need for being here. Focus. I fought for this country. And when it was won, the cowards who spent their lives trying to be white instead of fighting to remain true to their heritage, suddenly returned and gave it away again.

Ben   What are you talking about?

Buthelezi   I saw how you looked at her. It's not your fault. That's all you know.

Ben   You crazy! It's not like that!

Buthelezi   Have you looked closely at those handcuffs? I
know you've seen a certain kind of handcuffs – the movie ones
with a long chain. We don't use those kinds. No chain. Just
one small link between two solid metal cuffs. So once they
come on, you can't do anything.

*He lifts **Ben** to standing and reaches behind for the cuffs.*

Buthelezi   This is the truth of your life.

Ben   I'm nineteen! I was born after apartheid!

Buthelezi   No, no, no, no. You are not listening.

He grabs the cuffs and twists.

Ben *rises on to his toes, throwing his head forward, and screams.*

Buthelezi   That was a small twist. If I twist a little harder,
I could break both of your wrists without me sweating.

He twists again, lifting the cuffs higher.

Ben *practically has his head to his knees on tiptoe, arms high over his
head.*

Buthelezi   With a strong lift and a twist, I could dislocate
both of your shoulders. It's harder work for me, but the agony
you feel if I did that . . . ? (*Whistles*).

*He lets go and **Ben** drops to his knees.*

Ben   What would your father say if he saw you now?

Buthelezi   He would say: good evening, officer. And walk
on. So. Let us play a game. I will give you two chances. You
want to know why? Because I'm a nice guy. I'm not going to
break your wrists, or shoulders, that's not me. But I'm going to
see you dance. You know panesula?

Ben   No.

Buthelezi   Don't worry. It's in your blood. I'll bring it out of you. Masinga. *Shaye ye*[61] *music.*

Masinga, *who's been watching, lifts the music up.*

Buthelezi *grabs the cuffs and lifts again.*

Ben *rises from kneeling to standing.* **Buthelezi** *just gives the cuffs little twists whilst holding them up and high, which causes* **Ben** *to jump, skip and stay on his toes – similar to a pantsula style of dance.*

Skinn *is completely distraught, listening to this.*

Buthelezi *stops twisting.* **Ben** *drops to his knees again.*

Buthelezi   Hear that? It's your song.

Ben   You can't, you can't, what are you –

Buthelezi   You are Xhosa right? I don't think a Zulu man would forget his language but the Xhosa, who can say? Here is how it works: if you want me to stop, say: 'Officer Buthelezi I did not drink and drive. Please let me go.' I'm serious. You say that, I will stop and let you go.

Ben   Officer Buthelezi, I did not –

Buthelezi *twists the cuffs again.* **Ben** *can't help himself and screams as he launches himself into the air.*

Skinn   Oh Jesus, fuck, please, don't, don't, fuck!

Buthelezi *stops.*

Buthelezi   You are Xhosa, right? You must say it in Xhosa.

Skinn   Leave him alone you fucker!

Ben   I can't, I can't –

Buthelezi   You didn't think you could pantsula, look how I helped you. Let's see if we can get you to remember your mother tongue.

He twists the cuffs and **Ben** *has to pantsula again.*

61 Hit the . . .

Masinga *lights up a cigarette.*

Voice on Skinn's phone   You have run out of air time.

Skinn   No, no, no, please no!

Skinn's phone   Please recharge your account.

Lights fade out on **Skinn**.

Ben   Babba, Mfuwetu, babba please, nkhosi, amanzi, please, please stop, stop!

Buthelezi *lets go of the cuffs and* **Ben** *tumbles.* **Buthelezi** *takes a drag of* **Masinga**'s *cigarette.* **Masinga** *turns down the music.*

Buthelezi   You see? There's your Xhosa! We are getting somewhere.

Ben   No, stop –

Buthelezi   What's that?

Ben   Don't, please –

Buthelezi   It could take all night to get you to speak proper Xhosa. But I'm willing to help you.

Ben   Stop!

Buthelezi (*to* **Masinga**)   How disappointing. He doesn't want to learn isiXhosa.

Ben   You've . . . done this before.

Buthelezi   I was in the army. *Umkonto we Sizwe.*[62]

Ben   It's over, it's over, the war is over.

Buthelezi *lifts* **Ben** *to sitting position.*

Buthelezi   *A luta continua.* I hear that a lot.

Ben   Can I ask a question?

62 Spear of the Nation.

Buthelezi   Okay.

Ben   Did you ever – did you ever meet Mandela?

Buthelezi   No, I did not meet the commander in chief. And what does that matter? You people always go on about Mandela. Mandela, Mandela, Mandela! You think he fought the war by himself?

Ben   He would never have done this.

Buthelezi   There is a lot he would not do, that must be done.

Buthelezi *holds* **Ben** *close.*

Buthelezi   I can see you still don't get it. I did say I would give you two chances. Just say, in English if that's what you want. Just say: 'Officer Buthelezi I consent to having my blood tested.' Say it. Then we can get your blood, find you a nice cell and in the morning you can go home. Say it.

Ben *starts laughing uncontrollably.*

Masinga   What's so funny?

Ben   Apartheid . . . hasn't left. Afrikaaners . . . took off the uniform . . . you guys put it on. I guess that makes me a revolutionary.

He laughs hysterically. **Buthelezi** *indicates to* **Masinga** *to turn up the music.*

Buthelezi   No, my boy. No. You are not a revolutionary. You are just a pantsula dancer.

He twists the cuffs and **Ben** *starts dancing in agony.*

Suddenly the headlights of a car come up on them. The car slows to a stop, illuminating the scene:

Two cops in an empty lot, with an exhausted and crying prisoner hanging off the arms of one of them.

Buthelezi *whistles at* **Masinga**, *who steps forward to the lights, one hand on his gun and with the other waves to the driver to move on.*

All three watch intently to see what the lights will do.

The lights move on, plunging them back into the dark. **Masinga** *turns down the music.*

Masinga (*to* **Buthelezi**)   *U-Orion ak'siyon'induda enesineke.*[63]

Buthelezi (*to* **Ben**)   Masinga only cares about money. What do you think? Can we help him out?

Ben *mumbles to himself.*

Buthelezi   What's that you are saying?

Ben   I'm trying to remember my Xhosa.

Buthelezi *bursts out laughing.*

Buthelezi   That's good. That's real good.

He reaches for the cuffs again.

Masinga   Bhuti. It's an hour after midnight.

Buthelezi   I told you, after the blood test –

Masinga   And what about Tina?

He holds **Buthelezi**'s *present in his hands.*

Buthelezi *and* **Masinga** *exit.* **Ben** *is left alone on the floor, not moving. Above the moon shimmers with memories of other nights on the African soil.*

Scene Seven

Police office.

Skinn *enters the police station. She speaks to the audience as if they are the police.*

63 Orion isn't a very patient man.

Skinn   Hi. I need to speak to someone. It's an emergency. I know I shouldn't be here but the officer at the front desk couldn't help me.

Silence.

In fact he went for a smoke or something.

Silence.

A friend of mine has been taken by police officers and they're doing things to him.

Silence.

Violent things.

Silence.

What's wrong with you? Don't you hear me? They're torturing him right now!

Silence.

Look. You're the fucking police. You're supposed to help me.

Silence.

Shabangu *enters.*

Skinn   This is fuckin bullshit. They're killing him! Fucking do something!

Shabangu   Would you care to step into my office?

Skinn   Yes, thank you, yes. I'd like to report a crime.

Shabangu *indicates a chair.*

Shabangu   Sit down.

Skinn   I'd like to open a case.

Shabangu   Against who?

Skinn   A police officer.

Shabangu   On what charge?

Skinn Kidnapping.

Shabangu What's your name?

Skinn Skinn.

Shabangu Is that your surname or first name?

Skinn Both.

Shabangu Skinn Skinn?

Skinn Miss Skinn is fine for now.

Shabangu Do you have your ID book?

Skinn *takes her green ID book out.* **Shabangu** *reaches for it.* **Skinn** *pulls it away.*

Skinn Are you going to process the charges?

Shabangu It is highly unlikely that one of my officers would be party to a kidnapping –

Skinn It's one of your officers who pulled us over, took my friend. One of your officers said he was at Parkview but it was actually Linden, now I'm here but he is not, is he?

Shabangu Accusing someone, especially an officer, is a serious offence. Now as of this moment we are talking hypotheticals –

Skinn Talking what?

Shabangu Hypotheticals –

Skinn The fuck I am.

Shabangu Do you know what a hypothetical is?

Skinn *shakes her head.*

Shabangu It's a collection of ideas to get at a potential conclusion. Nothing is assumed true. It merely suggests a possible version of the truth.

Skinn Okay.

Shabangu   In my hypothetical, my officers are well trained and aware of the importance of operating within the law and with the community. It's a concept I have worked hard to instil in my patrol teams. We have good relations with the community. You have this idea that an officer, from here, has behaved unprofessionally.

Skinn   Kidnapped my friend.

Shabangu   Yes, but you see –

Skinn   That's not the only hypo-fuckin'-what's-it I'm talking about.

Shabangu   Okay.

Skinn   Ja, I'm also charging him with torture.

Shabangu   Let's, let's, let's not use . . . words like charging, charges or any other legal terminology that endeavours to . . . to . . . to concretise the discussion.

Skinn   Concretise?

Shabangu   Yes. Let's remain in the air, amongst ideas, engaging our assumptions on the matter.

Skinn   What are you talking about?

Shabangu   Hypotheticals.

Skinn   I heard him tortured on my phone! They didn't take his phone because they never arrested him! So what does that mean? That he was kidnapped! He is not in my car, not snuggled up in bed, he is fuckin' gone! Does that concretise your hypo-what's-its for you?

Shabangu   *Ungazo khuluma name kanjalo, wena!*[64] This is my house. I am not your *Nami.*[65]

Skinn   My nanny – ?

64 Do not speak to me that way.

65 Nanny.

Shabangu   Do you know why we speak in hypotheticals first? To allow a two-way communication to occur. But I can see you are no different to the people who raised you. You think you are automatically right. You own the truth, neh? So you can come in here to an officer and demand I do as you command.

Pause.

Skinn   I'm sorry. For my behaviour. Can we work this out? Please.

Shabangu   I will need your green Identity Book.

Skinn *lays her ID book on the table.*

Shabangu   I will lay the charges. But if your accusations are false, I will be forced to lay charges against you.

Skinn   That doesn't sound legal.

Shabangu   But it is. Perfectly legal. If you can substantiate your claims then you are within the law. So. Miss Skinn. Once that ID book is in my hands you cannot undo such actions.

He reaches for the ID book, which **Skinn** *intercepts.*

Skinn   I know one of their names.

Shabangu *(in disbelief)*   You are accusing more than one officer.

Skinn   I know his name. The one called the other Bhuti. He is a big man. Strong. Clean-shaven. Slow-moving, right? But not in a way that means he's slow. Dangerous is what I mean. You know who I'm talking about. He's the one called Bhuti.

Shabangu   And you are ready to lay charges against this . . . man?

Skinn   No.

Shabangu   No.

Skinn   No. No charges. I was speaking in hypo-what's-its.

Shabangu   Hypotheticals.

Skinn   Ja. Hypotheticals.

Shabangu   Anything else I can do for you?

Skinn   No.

Shabangu   If your friend is really with one of my officers, he is fine. They probably had to respond to a few calls before bringing him in. If you wait, they will be here soon and we can get to the bottom of this. You'll see. Everything's alright.

Skinn *leaves.*

Scene Eight

Shabangu *stands and calls* **Buthelezi**. *During the monologue we shift to* **Buthelezi** *listening to the message, shifting to* **James** *calling* **Skinn** *('Heart of Glass') shifting to* **Masinga** *calling his client ('Tkzee')* **Skinn** *calling* **Ben** *(ringtone).* **Ben** *is unmoving on the floor. All these calls intermingle to*

Lights up on the radio booth. **DJ Mavovo**, *the Neon Angel of the night dances.*

Shabangu   Bra Meli? Why is your phone always on silent? You better listen to this message and call me right back. There's a young girl, *womlungu,*[66] who came in here saying you kidnapped someone. Kidnapped! Of course I don't believe her. Because you would not do that. Not now not to me. Right? We go too far back. You know what I'm saying, Meli, this is important to me. If you decided to be reckless after I warned you about the public perception of us, how it's important we remain positive in the eyes of the public – you are messing with my life! *Awuyekel' ukuzi cabangela wedwa!*[67]

66 White person.

67 Don't be selfish, man, don't be thinking only of yourself.

Because should it blow up in your face, I won't be diving in front of you to take the bullets. I will be pulling the trigger at the public's command. Do you hear me, Melisizwe? You better get this message. You better answer me.

James (*overlapping*)   *Het ek dit verdien? Moenie stress van wat gebeur het nie. Wat van my? Wat van my? Miskien was dit jou skuld? Bel my terug asseblief.*[68] Don't be afraid.

Masinga (*also overlapping*)   No, no, it's not our intention to mislead you / we meant to go / It may not have worked out tonight but we can / we can / let's not / could you / could you listen to me / give me a moment /don't end this relationship!

Exit all except **Mavovo**, **Skinn** *and* **Ben**, *unmoving.*

Scene Nine

Radio booth. / Skin's car. / Police van. A neon sign of a sun. Two words are written on both sides: 'Sunrise Bar'. The sign slowly lights up, silhouetting **Skinn** *on her phone.*

DJ Mavovo   This is the Power and the Glory on 92.9. You're listening to DJ Mavovo, the eyes and ears of Jozi. Are you there, Mzansi? Are you still out? Awake and aware? The phone lines are open. Tell us your story. We got a caller on the line. Skinn, are you there?

Skinn   Mavovo!

DJ Mavovo   Who you partying with, what you doing?

Skinn   The party's been disrupted actually.

DJ Mavovo   I'm sure we can cure that, where are you?

68 Did I really deserve this? Pushing aside how you feel about what happened, what about me? Have you ever considered that you might be at fault here? That I'm the victim? Just think about it and get back to me.

Skinn My friend Ben has been kidnapped by the police.

DJ Mavovo What did you say?

Skinn He was shoved into the back of a police van and they took him somewhere.

DJ Mavovo Skinn, slow down. You're telling me your friend was arrested tonight.

Skinn No. Not arrested. Kidnapped.

DJ Mavovo Okay, that's new.

Skinn And then I heard them torturing him.

DJ Mavovo You do know this is a radio station –

Skinn My phone cut out, he isn't answering any more – I'm seriously worried they might kill him.

DJ Mavovo Woah, Skinn! Okay, wow. That's a pretty wild story. Kidnap, torture . . . murder? You don't hold back, do you?

Skinn You know I'm being serious here, right?

DJ Mavovo No, I don't actually know that. I don't know how you got past my producer, but if this were serious, you wouldn't be calling us.

Skinn Then who do you call when the police are up to shit?

DJ Mavovo This is a radio station.

Skinn A public radio station! Public!

DJ Mavovo We're going to cut to a commercial break –

Skinn (*overlapping*) We need help now! Everyone who has a car should drive out and look for two policemen with a prisoner. If spotted they can call me.

DJ Mavovo (*overlapping*) Girl, you are crazy.

Skinn Why you laughing? You think this is funny?

DJ Mavovo You're listening to 92.9 with DJ Mavovo.

Skinn   Don't you dare cut me off!

DJ Mavovo   We'll be right back.

Blackout on **Mavovo**.

Skinn *hangs up. Pulls a zap at the night sky.*

Skinn   FUCK YOU! Somebody please. Help me.

She phones **Ben**. **Ben***'s ringtone.* **Masinga** *comes in and lifts up* **Ben**, *uncuffing him. Places him in the back of the van.*

Ben *answers the phone.*

Ben   Skinn.

Skinn   Ben. Fuck, you okay? Where are you?

Ben   I don't know. Some township.

Skinn   Which one?

Ben   No idea.

Skinn   Well get some ideas. Tell me something I can use.

Ben   We visiting his wife. He called her Tina.

Skinn   Can you see a street address –

Ben   Can you play me a song?

Skinn   Huh?

Ben   It's quiet here . . . and . . . I can't . . . I can't think about it. Please.

Skinn   Okay. Sure. Any requests?

Ben   Anything but kwaito.

Skinn *plays 'Azukiiro No Kaori', followed by 'Tobiume', both by Susumu Yokota.*

The music brings them together onstage. They walk towards each other.

Ben   Where are you?

Skinn   By my car.

Ben *cries as quietly as he can.*

Skinn   Just give him what he wants.

Ben   What does he want?

Skinn   Your blood, give him your blood, that's what he wants, right?

Ben   Give him my blood.

Skinn   Fuck it, Ben! No one's going to be angry with you if you just give up! Give in! Get it over with! Then you can come home. Ben. This, this is a fuckin' mess, I'm sorry, but I can't fuckin' do this. I can't. This is not my thing.

Ben   Why'd you pick me up?

Skinn   What?

Ben   In the club. Why d'you ask me to come have a smoke in the car with you?

Skinn   I dunno –

Ben   You don't even know me.

Skinn   You looked like a nice guy.

Ben   A nice guy –

Skinn   Ja, a nice guy.

Ben   You like picking up nice guys.

Skinn   Fuckin' better than an asshole.

Ben   You should go home. Get some sleep.

Skinn   I picked you up 'cause I needed a place to stay. Okay? I saw you standing there, looking like you'd never had a dark day in your life. And I thought, this guy has a really soft bed somewhere.

Ben   You wanted to sleep on my bed.

Skinn   On your bed with its high walls, and private security and cameras, look, I just wanted to close my eyes for a while. You looked like you'd give up your bed for a quick cuddle.

Ben   I had other options. Dineo is probably still waiting for me at Duke's.

Skinn   Dineo, me, the cops. You're definitely getting fucked tonight. That was a joke.

Ben   Good one. Skinn, you gotta stay away from this.

Skinn   No.

Ben   You can't save me.

Skinn   Yes I can.

Ben   This man is trying to break me.

Skinn   We can do this together –

Ben   I can't do this and worry about you as well!

Skinn   You think I'm having a party over here? I've drawn out every rand I have, which is not much, I can tell you that. I've got problems of my own, but I'm sticking my neck out for you. For you Ben. Be grateful.

Ben   Grateful? You think I should be grateful? Why? Because you're white and you're making an effort? Go home. You don't owe me anything.

Skinn   Wait. I'm sorry, I just, we're both idiots here. Don't make it a race thing.

Ben   You can't get away from it Skinn. No one's born free any more.

Skinn   Bullshit. Stop trying to be a fucking martyr. I'm coming for you.

Ben   Skinn –

Skinn   I got a contact that will help. And by the way I'm not helping you because you're black. Don't ever say that to me again.

Ben   What's your real name?

Skinn *pulls back and lifts the phone to her ear.*

Skinn   I'll tell you. When I see you.

They stare at each other. **Ben** *lifts the phone to his ear again.*

Ben *hangs up.*

Skinn *hangs up.*

Scene Ten

Police van.

Masinga *sits in the front of the car, window rolled down.*

Ben *in the back.*

Masinga *jumps out of the front and goes to the van doors, unlocking them and swinging them open.*

Ben *looks up at him.*

Ben   He is going to kill me.

Masinga   He's not going to kill you. He's just having problems in his life.

Ben   That's funny. That's real funny. So I should feel okay knowing it's not personal. He just has issues. Why are the doors open?

Masinga   I'm going for a piss.

He walks away.

Ben *sits in the van. His hands are not cuffed and the door is open. No one is around.*

He moves towards the doors and looks out. He takes a step out. He stops. He draws it back in.

From the darkness we hear **Masinga**.

Masinga   Why aren't you leaving, cheeseboy?

Ben   Ben. My name is Ben.

Masinga   Why aren't you leaving?

Ben   It's called resisting arrest. I jump out. Run. You catch me and charge me for a real crime. All your actions seem justified, right?

Masinga *comes back, stands by the door.*

Masinga   We do not want to be here, alright?

Ben   And the form he signed for me?

Masinga   Don't worry about that.

Ben   I need to know what it's for.

Masinga   You should concentrate on doing what he asks of you –

Ben   What does that form say?!

Masinga   It's admission of guilt.

Ben   Guilty of what?

Masinga   Drunken driving.

Ben   It won't hold up in court.

Masinga   Exactly. So what's the problem? It's been a couple of hours. Even if we did the test now, it won't show any alcohol in your blood.

Ben   I wasn't drunk driving!

Masinga   Then just give him your blood and *sigaku prosesa, bes'uhambe uye ekhaya,* by the time *ifika eNkantolo, kuzutholakala ukuthi awunacala.*[69]

69 . . . We can process you then you can go home and when the court case comes you will be proved innocent and we can all get on with our lives!

Ben   I don't. Speak. That. Language.

Masinga   Co-operate.

Ben   He's been torturing me –

Masinga (*overlapping*)   We used necessary force so we could fulfil our duties as officers. It's our right to use force when facing individuals who do not comply with the law –

Ben (*overlapping*)   Necessary? You kidnapped me and tortured me in order to get me to agree with whatever fuckin' bullshit charge –

Masinga   You resisted arrest! You resisted what was asked of you! Give him what he wants!

Pause.

Ben   You like watching?

Masinga   Enough talking.

Ben   At least he is brave enough to stand for what he believes in.

Masinga   I've decided that I don't like you, cheeseboy.

Ben   I don't consider you a close friend either.

Masinga   You know why this man works night shift? So he doesn't have to fall asleep in the dark. Last time he did, he woke up screaming, took out his gun and shot every pillow in the house. Give him whatever he wants.

The front door opens. **Buthelezi** *comes out, his present in hand.*

Buthelezi   You can't keep me out of my own house! Are you just going to just stand there? Say something! I'm sorry. I am down on my knees! You have to believe that a man can change. We can fix this. We can see a therapist, like you suggested. Please. Tina. *Musu'kdinwa.*[70] You belong to me. You

70 Don't give up on me.

belong to me. You, Siphokazi, Nonto, Sinazo . . . you belong to me!

The door slams closed.

He throws the present at the door.

Cigarette.

Masinga *hands* **Buthelezi** *a cigarette.*

Buthelezi   Did he run?

Masinga   No. Bhuti . . . things have always been easy between us, you know? But the way you are acting . . . maybe we should just call it a night.

Buthelezi   We are not taking a delivery tonight.

Masinga   Bhuti, it's good pay and *umas'cala ukungenz' ama-delivery, bazothol' omuny' umuntu ozowenza.*[71]

Buthelezi   And where would we put it? *Lapha emuva? Lenale sdwedwe?*[72] You must be joking.

Masinga   Let's drop him at the police station, charge him and we can quickly get the delivery done.

Buthelezi   I'm sick of this shit. Everyone thinks they can tell me what to do. Do you even know what is in the package? And who is Orion anyway? We know nothing about him!

Masinga   Bhuti, it's just a job –

Buthelezi   A job?

Masinga   Relax, man –

Buthelezi   And this woman tells me I must leave my own house. To where!?

Masinga   Maybe the country.

71 If we start dropping deliveries someone else will take our place.

72 Back there? With him?

Buthelezi   Watch yourself, boy. Do you hear me, Masinga!?
I'm tired of this shit!

Ben   Problems with your wife?

Buthelezi   You're a fool, boy. What must your father think
of you?

Ben   Not much if he thinks of me at all.

Buthelezi   Why is that?

Ben   He left us to fight.

Buthelezi   He was a soldier. Did you look for him?

Ben   No.

Buthelezi   Why?

Ben   He chose to leave.

Buthelezi   Maybe he could not return.

Ben   He chose to leave.

Buthelezi   Are you ashamed of who you are?

Ben   Who I am is not defined by him or you.

Buthelezi   Who you are is completely defined by me! By
everyone who came before you! By what happened and what
we chose to do about it! We fought and died for your freedom.
Maybe your father paid the ultimate price and you don't care.
Look at you. So ready to give up the name your father fought
for.

Ben   It's my name too –

Buthelezi   It was given to you by the man you're too
ashamed to find. You would have his bones lie in an
unmarked grave. A forgotten man. That's his gift from you.

Ben   He chose –

Buthelezi   He had no choice! He fought so that you could
choose.

He brings his face right up to **Ben**'s.

Buthelezi   Give me your hand.

He takes **Ben**'s *hand, places it on his chest.*

Buthelezi   Do you feel it? The scar.

Ben *nods.*

Buthelezi   I walked the *Patria o Muerte*. The bridge to the fatherland or death. We had been trained in the Soviet Union, returned for final initiations in Angola, transferred to Zambia to cross the Zambezi river into Rhodesia to march under the cover of night and bush to South Africa. We were going to fight the war at home. On home soil, street by street! We travelled at night. Then one night I stopped to take a piss. I was thinking . . . I don't remember what I was thinking before the bullet hit me. One shot. I did not fall. Just kept pissing with a surprised look on my face. And this bush stands up, forming the shape of a man, lowering its gun. Two eyes stared at me. I don't know what I was thinking before the bullet, but after? I thought of my Tina that I would never see again, because of this bush. I didn't even zip up. I just took out my knife and stabbed that bush in the eye. Couldn't see it in the dark, but I felt it. Spraying on me. Soaking my hands. And it felt good. Eventually the bush stopped moving. I had a small flashlight. I shined my light on him, wiping the black paint he had on. I kept wiping it away, looking for that pink face. Black skin. There was only black skin. Gunfire. Screams. I sat down. Waited. Waited in the silence after the battle. I was fighting for freedom. What was he fighting for? Speak to me in your mother tongue and I will let you go.

Ben   I can't.

Buthelezi   You can't or you won't. Tell me your African name.

Ben   Somandla.

Buthelezi   Somandla! The Almighty! You should use that name.

Ben   Somandla is someone I used to be.

Buthelezi   And so we finally come to it. Ben belongs to America. Somandla belongs to Africa. Or are you a soutie?

Ben   A what?

Buthelezi   A soutie. A man with one foot in Africa, the other in America and his privates cooling in the ocean. (*Laughs.*) Go back to your country, Ben. But if you're going to stay, then speak with the voice of Somandla.

Ben   Do you know what happens when you lose your language? The world ceases to have shape. No shape no words no nothing nothing no thing. You are vanished. A ghost haunting a little boy's body. I was three years old when my mother took me overseas. I only spoke Xhosa then. No one else spoke that language. My mother wouldn't answer me. I couldn't remember the days. Only the nights. When everyone was asleep I'd hear voices. Are you a ghost? Are you really here?

Masinga   You broke him.

Ben   Only I can see your ghost. Maybe 'cause I died a little death once. You can see Somandla and Somandla sees you. Deadman. You died out there in the bush. You just won't accept it.

Buthelezi   I accept nothing. You think you can erase me? I am thousands of years old, Somandla! I am an unbroken chain of a people!

He strikes **Ben**.

Buthelezi   There's something breaking in me . . . and . . . and I don't know what I'm going to do. I'm going to do something terrible . . .

Masinga *steps forward.*

Masinga   Lieutenant. Shift is almost over. We have to wrap this up.

Buthelezi   Time to finish what we started.

Exit all.

Scene Eleven

Sunrise Bar.

Skinn *sits at a bar stool. Two glasses of whisky.*

James *enters.*

James   One of those jacks for me?

Skinn *slides one close to him.*

James   You had me going. Really. I was insane my bokkie, you should ask Trisha, I couldn't do nothing. Just pacing at the front door waiting.

Skinn   I need a favour.

James   Ja, okay. We can, uh, let's . . . Ja. What is it?

Skinn   There's this ou and he's in serious kak. Coupla kerels dropped him in the shit.

James   *Wat het hy gedoen?*[73]

Skinn   Hung out with me.

James *(laughs)*   That will do it. *Wat is sy naam?*[74]

Skinn   Ben.

James   Ben who?

Skinn   Uh . . . shit. An African name, I forgot.

James   A swart ou?

Skinn   Ja so? You got a problem with that?

73 What he do?

74 What's his name?

James   Chill.

Skinn   I don't need shit from you now.

James   What, your broekies too tight?! Relax. So a swart ou named Benjamin.

Skinn   Can you do something about it?

James   What's the names of those kerels?

Skinn   Dunno. They told me Parkview police station but they in Linden but they not there and *Ben bel my heeltyd omdat die kak bly uit hom geskop word. Kan jy help?*[75]

James   Alright. Calm down, my bokkie –

Skinn   Kan jy help?!

James   Ja, I've got a contact in the police. I can put in a word for him. Alright?

Skinn   Thanks.

James   Sure. That's what a man does. Helps his lady. You really had me going. Sweatin' bullets, yessis man. But that's over now. We sort out this friend of yours then it's all lekker again eh?

Silence.

The other girls miss you. I spoke to Lolly, he said it's okay. Practically begged him. On my knees and everything. He says you can work the bar only. No floor work.

Skinn   Ja. No thanks. I got a thing going.

James   *Natuulik. Dis jou lewe.*[76] Got to keep moving up. Improve yourself like you said. I get that.

Skinn   I'm not coming back to you, James.

75 I keep getting phone calls from Ben as he's getting the shit kicked out of him. Can you help?

76 Course. It's your life.

James   I was angry, a little high –

Skinn   Let's not fuckin' do this –

James   Where's your Christian spirit, man?

Skinn   You punched me in the face!

James   And I'm sorry! Okay?

Skinn   Ja. But once a guy like you tastes blood, nothing's quite as sweet.

Pause.

James   Your ouballie called looking for you.

Skinn   My pa? Looking for me?

James   Ja.

Skinn   If that fuckin' skelm is up to shit, fuck it. *Ek Gee n' fok nie.*[77]

James   Ja, well, you better fokken give a shit alright? I had to listen to him screaming for money or else he's gonna tell everyone I slept with his sixteen-year-old daughter.

Skinn   Come off it, James. As if you didn't know that.

James   You said you was eighteen!

Skinn   Ja! So I could work at the bar! And drive a car! When you picked me up I was in my school uniform with a backpack.

James   Ja, fine, whatever, look he's threatening to call the cops on me –

Skinn   So go punch him in the face.

James   You ever gonna let that go?

Skinn   No.

James   *Ek is nie jou pa nie, weet jy?*[78]

77 I don't give a shit.

78 I'm not your father, you know.

Skinn   Ja. And you're not my boyfriend neither. Call your contact.

James   Let's enjoy our fuckin' drink first.

Silence.

You're amazing. A real fuckin' ball-buster. I offer you my home, let you drive my wheels – speaking of wheels, I want my fuckin' car back.

Skinn   I'll bring it to you tomorrow. Promise.

Pause.

James   Fuck this. You want my help, it doesn't come for free.

Skinn   You said you was gonna do it –

James   That was before, ja? Before I knew you was planning to leave me. You want something from me, I want something from you.

Skinn *gets up.*

Skinn   Ja. Okay, James.

James   Woah, we going already?

Skinn   You're not gonna do it.

James   I'm gonna do it.

Skinn   No you're not.

James   Let's have another round on me.

Skinn   Bye, James.

James *grabs* **Skinn**.

James   Hold on.

Skinn   Let go of me!

James   Easy now.

Skinn   I said let go!

James   Let's be civil –

Skinn   Fuck you!

James   Skinn –

Skinn   Fuck off!

James   Chill!

Skinn   Help! Somebody get this asshole off me –

James *strikes* **Skinn**.

James   I said chill, man!

Skinn *falls to the floor.* **James** *turns to the audience hands held up, apologetic.*

James   Sorry folks, sorry. Personal matter. We just, uh, we just talking things out. Get back to your drinks.

(*To a specific audience member.*) Hey, mind your own business man! Don't cause kak here. I don't come to your fuckin' home do I?

(*To* **Skinn**.) Look at what you made me do. You call me here to make me do something for you. And you treat me like, like I'm nothing? Me? Nothing? You can't treat people that way, you can't. Ah shit, I just. Bokkie. Look I'm sorry, I just, you got me all angry again. I can't take it, you know? I can take most things, but not this. Not this, Skinn. You know, who took it for you when Lolly was angry with you about that money you stole? Me, that's who. I pulled your ass out of the fire! And I would do it again. I'd do anything for you, my bokkie. When you finally went home with me that night, Skinn baby. It was great. It was good. I remember everything. You gonna throw all that away? Wasn't it great? Hey? I'm trying to say that I love you. You get that? Hey? Come here let me –

Skinn *gets up quickly, pulls back from* **James**.

James   Skinn, wait. Come on.

Skinn *punches* **James**.

Skinn You don't even know my real name.

James You fuck him?

Skinn What?

James You fuck him?

She exits.

A fuckin swart ou! *Jy het my vir a swart ou vokken gelos vokken bitch!* [79]

Scene Twelve

Dr Pravesh*'s office.*

Ben *sits on a chair in the doctor's office, his hands cuffed.* **Buthelezi** *and* **Masinga** *stand next to him.*

Pravesh *enters. There's blood on her uniform. She lights up a cigarette right there.*

Pravesh You're back. What time is it now? 3:47. Have you spent the evening with this one?

Buthelezi It's an important case.

Pravesh Must be. Wish I could concentrate on a single patient with a head cold.

Buthelezi There are certain details of the case you are not aware of –

Pravesh *kills the cigarette.*

Pravesh I was kidding, officer. You've come to an agreement, yes?

Buthelezi Yes, we have.

79 You fuckin left me for a black man, fuckin bitch!

Pravesh   Good. Let's make this quick.

Pravesh *takes out a fresh pair of latex gloves, puts them on.*

Buthelezi   Mr Mthombeni what do you have to say?

Long pause. From here on **Ben** *looks only at* **Buthelezi**.

Ben   He taught me how to pantsula.

Pravesh   What?

Ben   Pantsula dance. Everybody's doing it.

Pravesh   What the hell is he talking about?

Masinga   Mr Mthombeni do you consent to having your blood –

Ben (*to* **Buthelezi**)   I see you.

Buthelezi   Do you consent –

Ben   And I love you.

Pravesh   Officer, I can't take his blood –

Ben   I love you.

Buthelezi   Doctor, please wait –

Ben   I love you.

Buthelezi   Do you consent, Somandla!

Ben   I love you, brother –

Buthelezi *grabs* **Ben** *by the throat, lifting him off the chair.*

Buthelezi   SHUT UP!

Ben   I love you!

Buthelezi *starts choking* **Ben**, *who struggles to get away from him.*

Buthelezi   MASINGA, HOLD HIM!

Ben   I love you!

Masinga *is frozen to the spot.*

Buthelezi   MASINGA!

*Masinga rushes over and pins **Ben***'s *arms against his sides.*
Buthelezi** lifts **Ben** above them, never taking his eyes from **Ben's *eyes.* ***Ben** stares back, but as he loses oxygen his struggles increase, causing **Masinga** to hold him tighter.*

*And **Pravesh***'s *phone beeps. She takes it out of her pocket and reads the SMS.* ***Ben***'s *struggles intensify in a crescendo.*

Masinga   Buthelezi, stop!

Pravesh *starts SMSing back.*

*And **Ben** freezes, his body rigid in the air, staring deep into **Buthelezi***'s *eyes. He goes limp.*

Masinga   Buthelezi!

Buthelezi *pulls back.* **Masinga** *drops **Ben**, who lies there.*

Pravesh *stops smiling and looks down at **Ben**.*

Buthelezi *holds up his hand to her.*

He grabs the cuffs and twists.

Ben *wakes up screaming, struggling to escape the pain from the cuffs.*

He is a blubbering wreck.

Ben   I consent I consent I consent please I consent –

Buthelezi   Doctor.

Pravesh   Sit him down.

She takes out a sealed medical kit.

Buthelezi *and **Masinga** lift **Ben** back on to the chair.*

Pravesh   Mr Mthombeni do you consent to having your blood tested?

*Before **Ben** can speak **Buthelezi** twists the handcuffs slightly.* ***Ben** screams:*

Ben   I CONSENT! I CONSENT!

Pravesh   This is a police blood test kit. Do you admit it hasn't been tampered with?

Ben   No it hasn't no no it hasn't it hasn't −

Pravesh *opens the kit.*

Pravesh   Please relax. It will make it easier to get the blood sample.

She takes the sample. Everyone watches as the blood slowly fills the syringe.

Ben   Doctor. I just. I just. How? How do you just watch?

Pravesh   A man comes in with a woman in his arms, stab wound to the chest. And he's crying, begging me to save her life. He loves her he says. Anyway. She lives. Sometime later, a year maybe, she's brought in again, but it's too late for her. He's still crying 'Save her.' He stabbed her. She chose not to press charges. And he stabbed her again. They taught me a very important lesson.

Ben   What?

Pravesh   To mind my own business. My job is to patch you up and send you back out there.

The syringe is full. She takes out the needle and repacks the kit.

Do you admit the kit has been properly sealed and not tampered with?

Ben *nods.*

Buthelezi *steps forward.*

Ben   Yes, it's perfect, everything is perfect, perfect.

Pravesh *gets up, ripping off the latex gloves.*

Pravesh (*to* **Buthelezi**)   I'll send it for testing first thing Monday morning. Unless there is a particular rush?

Masinga   No. No rush. Monday is fine.

Pravesh *exits.*

Masinga   Buthelezi. *Ungahamba ngizocedelela.*[80]

Buthelezi   He's my prisoner –

Masinga   *Ngithe ngizocedelela!*[81]

Buthelezi *backs away.*

Scene Thirteen

Linden police station.

Ben *sits with* **Masinga**.

There is only the addition of a door to the one side, open and full of light. **Ben** *stares at the open door.*

Masinga   I've got your paperwork in order here. Did they give you something to eat? In the cells?

Ben *nods.*

Masinga   Yes. Well. I wrote here that you have been accused of drinking and driving. That and the blood sample makes the case. But don't worry, I don't think it will hold in court. Do you want to read it?

Ben *shakes his head.*

Masinga   You can add whatever you think is relevant. You don't have to worry about him any more. He got what he wanted. I . . . am sorry. About what my partner did.

He orders his papers and lifts a pen to **Ben**.

Skinn *appears, standing in the light. Waiting.* **Ben** *stares at her.*

Masinga   All I need is your signature here. Mr Mthombeni? Ben. Ben, are you paying attention?

80 I will handle it.

81 I said I will handle it!

Ben *picks up the pen. He struggles to sign it; has to hold his one wrist with the other.*

Masinga   I'm going to do you a favour. I'm setting your court case one year from now. Between now and then do you know how many cases we go through? So many that we can't handle them all. This case file will be buried under a mountain of unsolved cases. By this time next year, it will be as if it never happened. Doesn't that sound good? Well?

Ben *nods.*

Shabangu *appears, dressed in civilian clothes.*

Masinga (*nods*)   I think that's everything. Let me make you a copy.

He gets up.

Shabangu   Masinga. The celebration's been scheduled for this Tuesday afternoon. I got you off shift, if you still coming.

Masinga   Of course.

Shabangu   How was the night?

Masinga   I'd like to be redeployed. Now that you are Sector Commander. I'd like a day shift. I'm not cut out for the night.

Shabangu   Want to talk about it?

Masinga   Not officially, no.

Shabangu   Alright.

Masinga *exits.*

Shabangu (*looks to* **Skinn**)   You can come in if you want.

Skinn *shakes her head, no.*

Buthelezi *enters, dressed in civilian clothing.*

Shabangu (*pointing to* **Ben**)   This the one?

Skinn *nods.*

Shabangu   He looks alright to me. Seems you worried for nothing.

He turns to **Buthelezi**.

Shabangu   Lieutenant.

Buthelezi   Sector Commander.

Shabangu   *Uyilungisil' indadba yakho nenkosi-kazi?*[82]

Buthelezi   It's sorted.

Shabangu   And?

Buthelezi   You can file the order. I won't fight it.

Shabangu   Good. Anything else happen last night?

Buthelezi   Nothing unusual.

Shabangu   Good. Good.

He looks at **Ben**, *then at* **Skinn**.

Shabangu (*to* **Buthelezi**)   If anything happened last night I won't be able to protect you.

Buthelezi   I understand.

Shabangu   *Hamba Krahle*[83] Shenge.

Buthelezi   *Hamba Krahle* Shabangu.

Shabangu *exits.*

Buthelezi   Mr Mthombeni –

Ben *gets up and moves away from* **Buthelezi**.

Buthelezi   Hold on.

Ben   I'm leaving.

82 Have you sorted out your woman problem?

83 Go well.

Buthelezi I know, I know. I just . . . need to ask you. Last night. You said something. You said –

Ben I love you.

Buthelezi (*physically reacts*) Ja. Why did you say that?

Ben When I was in the back of the van I asked, why was this happening to me? You know what I heard? Nothing.

Buthelezi (*confused by* **Ben**) Ja, okay. But why did you say, huh –

Ben Nothing answered. Nobody was listening. Just darkness. It said I couldn't save myself. Money couldn't save me. Education couldn't save me. My skin couldn't save me. My name . . . couldn't save me. I had to sit there with the darkness and recognise that. Then I said the thing I was most afraid of. I said, 'This man is going to kill me.' That's when I understood what you meant by this.

He puts his wrists together.

Behind your name. Behind your skin. When you close your eyes. What's there?

Buthelezi Nothing.

Ben Yeah. Nothing. Behind everything you think you are, there is the darkness and the silence.

Buthelezi (*irritated*) Why did you say 'I love you'?

Ben *pulls his wrists apart.*

Ben So you could hear the darkness answer you.

Pause.

Buthelezi *Foetsak. Foetsak! Phuma la mfana.*[84]

Masinga *enters.*

---

84 Piss off. Piss off! Get out of here, boy.

*He hands **Ben** his report.*

Ben *takes the paper, and walks to the light and **Skinn**.*

He stops an arm's length from her.

Buthelezi *looks at **Masinga**, who turns away and exits.*

Skinn   Ben.

Ben (*joking*)   I'm hungry. You hungry? I feel so hungry. I could eat the world –

Skinn *reaches out to hug him.* **Ben** *pulls away distraught.*

Skinn *never stops touching him. She touches his face, his chest, his arms as he trembles to quiet.*

Ben (*his control breaking down*)   No! Don't touch me, don't touch me. Don't don't don't, okay? Not yet, please, Please just, just don't please, not, I can't not not not, no not here, I can't, I just I just I just, someone, please, Skinn, please help me –

Skinn   Ben. Ben. It's okay, Ben. It's okay Ben. Come back. Don't be afraid. Come back, Ben. Come back, come back to me, come back. I'm here. I'm with you. Okay?

Ben   What's your real name?

Skinn   Yve. Yvette Skinner.

Ben   My name is Somandla.

Skinn   Somandla.

*All the while **Buthelezi** watches. The scene fades, leaving **Buthelezi** alone on the stage, staring at the faded image of **Skinn** and **Ben**.*

*The moon rises up, flickering like an old TV set. From behind the lights of a car strike **Buthelezi**, illuminating him. He looks back at it – before he is plunged into darkness.*

End.

Bloomsbury Methuen Drama Modern Plays

include work by

Bola Agbaje	Robert Holman
Edward Albee	Caroline Horton
Davey Anderson	Terry Johnson
Jean Anouilh	Sarah Kane
John Arden	Barrie Keeffe
Peter Barnes	Doug Lucie
Sebastian Barry	Anders Lustgarten
Alistair Beaton	David Mamet
Brendan Behan	Patrick Marber
Edward Bond	Martin McDonagh
William Boyd	Arthur Miller
Bertolt Brecht	D. C. Moore
Howard Brenton	Tom Murphy
Amelia Bullmore	Phyllis Nagy
Anthony Burgess	Anthony Neilson
Leo Butler	Peter Nichols
Jim Cartwright	Joe Orton
Lolita Chakrabarti	Joe Penhall
Caryl Churchill	Luigi Pirandello
Lucinda Coxon	Stephen Poliakoff
Curious Directive	Lucy Prebble
Nick Darke	Peter Quilter
Shelagh Delaney	Mark Ravenhill
Ishy Din	Philip Ridley
Claire Dowie	Willy Russell
David Edgar	Jean-Paul Sartre
David Eldridge	Sam Shepard
Dario Fo	Martin Sherman
Michael Frayn	Wole Soyinka
John Godber	Simon Stephens
Paul Godfrey	Peter Straughan
James Graham	Kate Tempest
David Greig	Theatre Workshop
John Guare	Judy Upton
Mark Haddon	Timberlake Wertenbaker
Peter Handke	Roy Williams
David Harrower	Snoo Wilson
Jonathan Harvey	Frances Ya-Chu Cowhig
Iain Heggie	Benjamin Zephaniah

For a complete listing of Bloomsbury
Methuen Drama titles, visit:

www.bloomsbury.com/drama

Follow us on Twitter and keep up to date
with our news and publications
@MethuenDrama